MENTIA   L
ake   l   o

POLICY AND PRACTICE IN HEALTH AND SOCIAL CARE

POLICY AND PRACTICE IN HEALTH AND SOCIAL CARE
SERIES EDITORS
JOYCE CAVAYE and ALISON PETCH

Dementia and Well-being:
Possibilities and Challenges

Dr Ailsa Cook

Lecturer, Centre for the Older Person's Agenda
Queen Margaret University, Edinburgh

DUNEDIN

Published by
Dunedin Academic Press Ltd
Hudson House
8 Albany Street
Edinburgh EH1 3QB
Scotland

ISBN: 978-1-903765-76-0
ISSN 1750-1407

British Library Cataloguing in Publication data
A catalogue record for this book is available from the British Library

Typeset by Makar Publishing Production
Printed and bound in Great Britain by CPod

Contents

Series Editors' Introduction

Increasingly, the needs of people with dementia have been recognised as a key policy area during the past decade. At the time of going to press, in 2008, dementia has been identified as a national priority in Scotland, while in England a National Dementia Strategy has been launched. Prioritising the needs of individuals with dementia is essential as the numbers likely to live with the condition increase. Equally important is transformation from the traditional perception of a 'heart-sink' diagnosis to the promotion of a culture of dementia and well-being.

The concept of 'well-being' features prominently in current policy discourse. It is a concept that sounds intrinsically attractive but which in practice often proves rather more elusive. If this is true in general, it is likely to be even more the case for people experiencing dementia. Ailsa Cook adopts the notion of people leading healthy lives engaged in local communities as the basis for her translation of 'well-being'. She argues that any goal of well-being cannot be achieved without the active engagement of policy makers. She explores four key areas in detail: the promotion of health, of independence, of choice and control, and of social inclusion. Within each of these areas she presents a measured analysis, drawing on the emerging evidence base, and weighing both the barriers and the opportunities for implementing a goal of well-being. Wherever possible the arguments are based on the emerging research on what is important to people with dementia and the increasing knowledge of the policy and practice drivers that can support the achievement of well-being. A number of examples are also given illustrating imaginative ways in which support can be provided to demonstrate that dementia and well-being need not, and should not, be irreconcilable concepts.

Dr Joyce Cavaye
Faculty of Health and Social Care,
The Open University in Scotland,
Edinburgh

Professor Alison Petch
*Director, **research in practice** for*
adults*, Dartington Hall Trust,*
Totnes, Devon

Acknowledgements

I am grateful to many people for help, both direct and indirect, while writing this book. This book draws on ideas developed over a number of research projects and in collaboration and discussion with numerous colleagues, in particular Emma Miller, Alison Petch, Gill Hubbard, Heather Wilkinson, Susan Tester, Wendy Hulko, Dot Weaks, Murna Downs, Charlotte Clarke, John Keady and Margaret Whoriskey and colleagues at the Joint Improvement Team. I would like to thank my colleagues at the Centre for the Older Person's Agenda for supporting this process and in particular Julie Ferguson for her help retrieving materials. Many thanks also to my editors and to the anonymous reviewers for their very useful comments.

I have received considerable support in writing this book from my family and friends and would like to thank them all, but particularly Alex, Oscar, Mum and Dad.

This book and the arguments within it have been profoundly influenced by the stories of the many individuals with dementia and their carers whom I interviewed in the course of my research. I would like to thank all those who have given up their time and shared their experiences so willingly.

Ailsa Cook, Edinburgh, July 2008

Glossary of Abbreviations

DCM   Dementia Care Mapping
HEAT   Health Efficiency Access Treatment (health board performance management target)
ICP   Integrated Care Pathway
ISD   Information and Statistics Division (Scotland's national organisation for health information statistics)
MSP   Member of the Scottish Parliament
NICE   National Institute for Health and Clinical Excellence (the independent English organisation responsible for providing national guidance on promoting good health and preventing and treating ill health)
NSF   National Service Framework
SDWG   Scottish Dementia Working Group
SIGN   Scottish Intercollegiate Guidelines Network (the organisation that develops clinical guidelines for Scotland)
SPARRA Scottish Patients at Risk of Readmission and Admission

Preface

Over the past twenty years significant shifts in health and social care policy across the UK[1] have transformed the lives of many adults with disabilities and physical and mental health problems. The remit for health and social care services has been extended beyond providing just basic treatment and support and their role in supporting the well-being of service users and their carers is now explicitly recognised in policy. Specifically, well-being was headlined in the 2005 English Green Paper on social care *Independence, Well-being and Choice* (Department of Health, 2005a), and is identified as one of four high-level outcomes in the Scottish National Outcomes Framework for Community Care. All health and social care partnerships in Scotland are now directed to working towards delivering these outcomes for service users and their carers (Joint Future Unit, 2007).

This focus on well-being is reflected in the rafts of policy and legislation following the 1990 National Health Service and Community Care Act that have enabled many individuals, previously condemned to live out their lives in institutions, to move into independent accommodation in the community. Policy has sought to remove the barriers that many people face in accessing mainstream health services and to encourage people to live healthy lives engaged with their local communities (e.g. *Adding Life to Years*, Scottish Executive, 2002). Most recently, policy makers have demonstrated their commitment to mainstreaming new models of commissioning and providing individualised packages of care that give service users choice and control over the care they receive (e.g. *Our Health, Our Care, Our Say*, Department of Health, 2006). There is, however, a growing body of evidence that people with dementia are being excluded from many of these initiatives and are not getting the attention from policy makers that the condition deserves. This, it has been argued, has been a key challenge to improving well-being for people with dementia and has led the Alzheimer's societies in both England and Scotland to call upon their respective governments to make dementia a priority.

It is welcome, therefore, that in 2007 both administrations responded to these calls and announced that they were developing specific programmes of policy for dementia to be launched in 2008. In Scotland, dementia was identified as a national priority from 2008 in *Better Health, Better Care* (Scottish Government, 2007) and in England the first National Dementia

Strategy was launched in October 2008. Identifying dementia as a priority or developing a strategy is not, however, enough to guarantee improved well-being for people with dementia. If the policies are to make a difference to the well-being of people with dementia they must be grounded in a thorough understanding of what dementia is and what it is like to live with the condition and must be implemented with respect to the experiences and concerns of people with dementia at every stage of the condition. Furthermore, they need to be delivered in the context of a broader health and social care policy agenda that includes people with dementia. It is only then that the improvements seen for other groups of service users and their carers might also be realised for people with dementia.

The aim of this book is to contribute to academic debate around policy and dementia and to inform the development and implementation of policy for dementia by critically analysing recent and proposed rafts of policy in the light of their potential to impact on the well-being of people with dementia. Specifically the book:

- examines dementia-specific and general health and social care policy;
- reviews policy from both Scotland and England;
- reviews policy in the light of research evidence as to what is important in life to people with dementia and what supports their well-being;
- reviews policy in the context of theoretical understandings of what it is like to have dementia and what the major threats to the well-being of people with dementia are.

In so doing, the book addresses a vital gap in the academic literature on dementia and constitutes a useful resource for those seeking to develop and implement policy to make a difference to the lives of people with dementia, as well as for those studying and researching the condition.

The main part of the book is organised into four chapters, each one addressing an issue identified as important to the well-being of people with dementia by policy makers and people with dementia alike. These are: health, independence, choice and control, and social inclusion. First, however, the following chapter sets the scene for the rest of the book by defining the key concepts underpinning the book, dementia and well-being, and by considering the broader policy context.

Note

1. While health and social care policy is devolved across the UK and the specifics of individual policies discussed in this book may not apply directly to readers in Wales and Northern Ireland, there are many similarities between these and other post-

industrialised nations in terms of the provision of support to people with dementia meaning that the research and overall analyses presented are applicable across the UK and beyond.

CHAPTER 1

Definitions and Context

Dementia is the term used to describe a range of conditions that lead to a progressive decline in cognitive functioning. Dementia is predominantly, but not exclusively, a condition experienced by older people, with one in five people over the age of 80 having a form of dementia. Much less commonly, dementia can occur among working age adults. This is referred to as early onset dementia and accounts for 2.2% of all people with dementia in the UK (Knapp *et al.*, 2007).

Dementia is caused by a number of conditions, most commonly Alzheimer's disease and vascular dementia, but also less common conditions such as dementia with Lewy bodies, frontotemporal dementia, Creutzfeldt-Jakob disease, and AIDS-related dementia (Holden and Stokes, 2002). Scientific understanding as to the causes of dementia is still limited and, although recent research has identified a range of biological mechanisms underpinning the development of dementia, there is as yet no one clear explanation for the cause of dementia (Ritchie and Lovestone, 2002). A key practical consequence of the limitations of scientific understanding of the condition is that there are at present no definitive diagnostic tests for dementia and drug treatment options are limited.

The symptoms of dementia are diverse. They affect individuals' memory, reasoning and communication skills and impact on their ability to complete a wide range of everyday activities. Furthermore, people with dementia may experience psychological or behavioural difficulties as a consequence of their impairments and the disorientation and confusion they experience (Holden and Stokes, 2002). It is important to note, however, that people with dementia experience the condition in many different ways, influenced by the nature of damage in their brain, but also by their strengths, abilities and preferences throughout life, and a range of psychological, interpersonal and societal factors (e.g. Cantley and Bowes, 2004; Hulko, 2002; Kitwood, 1997).

Over the years many researchers, in particular those working from biomedical and neuropsychological perspectives, have sought to describe and delineate the deficits of dementia so that they could distinguish people with dementia from the 'normal' population. This research has often characterised dementia in relation to three stages — early, moderate and late stage dementia — and while this 'stage' model of dementia is of limited utility when thinking about the experiences of any individual with dementia, it does provide a useful snapshot for policy makers seeking to plan for the needs of a whole population of people with dementia. The National Audit Office (2007) report summarises these stages as follows:

Early stage symptoms often attributed to bereavement, stress or normal ageing:

- loss of short term memory;
- confusion, poor judgement, unwillingness to make decisions;
- anxiety, agitation or distress over perceived changes and inability to manage everyday tasks.

Middle stage symptoms

- more support required including reminders to eat, wash and use the lavatory;
- increasingly forgetful and may fail to recognise people;
- distress, aggression and anger are not uncommon, perhaps due to frustration;
- risks include wandering and getting lost, leaving the taps running or forgetting to light the gas;
- may behave inappropriately, e.g. leave the house in night clothes;
- may experience hallucinations.

Late stage symptoms include:

- inability to recognise familiar people, surroundings or places, though there may be flashes of recognition;
- increasing physical frailty, may start to shuffle or walk unsteadily, eventually becoming confined to a bed or wheelchair;
- difficulty eating and sometimes swallowing, weight loss, incontinence and gradual loss of speech.

Given the nature of the symptoms of dementia, it is not surprising that most people with dementia (more than 90%) rely on others to support them with day-to-day activities, and as the condition advances people's care needs increase (Melzer *et al.*, 2004). A considerable proportion of the support that people with dementia need comes from informal, unpaid carers (Alzheimer Scotland, 2007a); however, people with dementia are also significant users of health and social care services, relying on primary, secondary and social care (National Institute for Health and Clinical Excellence/ Social Care Institute for Excellence, 2006). There are currently

700,000 people with dementia across the UK and that number is expected to rise to over 1 million by the year 2021 (Knapp *et al.*, 2007). As a result, dementia constitutes a considerable cost to society, and a recent report estimates that the total cost of dementia to the UK is about £17 billion per year (Knapp *et al.*, 2007). It is important to note, however, that input from health and social care services constitutes a relatively small part of these costs, 23% in total, with unpaid carers absorbing 36% of the cost of care, and the cost of providing accommodation to people with dementia being 41%. This has been calculated by Knapp *et al.* as equating to an average annual cost of £25,472 to support an older person with dementia; the figure rises as the dementia progresses and reaches just over £31,000 a year if the person moves to a care home.

Despite the investment in care and support for people with dementia, there is extensive evidence that, to date, health and social care organisations have not risen to the challenge and that care services for people with dementia are inadequate, both in terms of the quality and extent of provision. Most recently, the National Audit Office report *Improving Services and Support for People with Dementia* (2007) raised concerns about the limited extent to which people with dementia can access basic services from diagnostic services to domiciliary care, as well as about the quality of services they receive. They concluded that dementia services do not deliver good value to the taxpayer, people with dementia or their carers. These findings echo those from the report by Derek Wanless (2006) on the future of social care services for older people and recent reports from both the Alzheimer's Society (Knapp *et al.*, 2007) and Alzheimer Scotland (2007a), all of which highlight the poor provision of services for people with dementia and their carers.

A key consequence of the failure of the system to provide adequate support is that levels of well-being among people with dementia and their carers are low. Not only is depression common among both groups (Burns *et al*, 1990; Papastavrou *et al.*, 2007), but researchers speaking to people with dementia have found that the poor quality of care that many people with dementia receive can have a profound impact on an individual's sense of self and self worth (e.g. Kitwood, 1997; Sabat, 2001). Indeed Brooker (2007, p. 32) summarised what it feels like to be on the receiving end of much current dementia care as follows:

> Incomplete assessments, no one contacting you when they promised, feeling deceived, the withholding of information, the over-prescribing of drugs you don't need and under-prescribing of ones that you do. Lack of privacy, indignity, insensitivity, disrespect, stigmatisation, disempowerment and boredom are all very familiar features to service users and their families. The erosion of

human and legal rights, and the overwhelming feeling that nothing personal is sacred, is still the day-to-day experience of people with dementia and their families.

The prevalence of dementia and the associated costs of providing care, not to mention the problems with dementia services and the subsequent impact on well-being, all make dementia a significant issue for health and social care policy. It is concerning, therefore, that until this year the issue of dementia had been largely ignored by policy makers in both England and Scotland. Furthermore, there is very little academic writing from the field of dementia that engages substantially with policy, apart from discussion of specific issues, such as legislation on incapacity (e.g. Mason and Wilkinson, 2002). Indeed Brooker, in response to her appraisal of the situation of people with dementia called for front line workers to improve the quality of life for people with dementia through their own practice, arguing that the implementation of government policy, such as the Single Shared Assessment process, will make little difference. While it is clearly essential that every individual involved in the care of people with dementia works to the best of their ability to improve the well-being of people with dementia, the central premise of this book is that significant changes to well-being will not be realised without the engagement of policy makers. Therefore, the aim of this book is to start to address the gap in the literature by critically examining the potential of both general and dementia-specific policy to improve well-being. Later in this chapter the overall policy context in relation to promoting well-being of users of health and social care services generally and people with dementia specifically is reviewed and key reasons why policy makers have tended to ignore dementia to date discussed. First, however, the concept of well-being is defined and key research relating to the well-being of people with dementia is reviewed.

Defining well-being

Before examining the research literature on well-being for people with dementia, it is important to define what is meant by the term well-being. Despite the prominence of well-being in policy, there is a distinct lack of conceptual clarity about what the term means and in particular how it relates to other concepts such as health and quality of life. This is unsurprising given that the broader literature on well-being, life satisfaction and quality of life is itself beset with contradictions and inconsistencies. In her review of conceptual models of well-being and quality of life, Galloway (2006) highlighted that the two terms are frequently used interchangeably and that there is a lack of consensus as to which domains should be included within each concept. Furthermore, there is disagreement within the literature as to the place of subjective experience within both concepts (Haas, 1999).

In seeking to clarify the field, Haas (1999) draws a distinction between well-being and quality of life. She argues that when your appraisal of a person's life is drawn entirely from their own perspective, then you are capturing well-being, as opposed to quality of life, which must include some objective measures of experience, for example health, income and functioning. Eckersley defines well-being as being 'about having meaning in life, about fulfilling our potential and feeling that our lives are worthwhile' (Eckersley, 2008, p. 3). He goes on to say:

> All in all, well-being comes from being connected and engaged, from being enmeshed in a web of relationships and interests. These give meaning to our lives. We are deeply social beings. The intimacy, belonging and support provided by close personal relationships seem to matter most; and isolation exacts the highest price.

Well-being, as defined in this way, is a very useful concept for thinking about the lives of vulnerable service users, such as people with dementia, as it neither prescribes what constitutes a good life, nor precludes the possibility for well-being on the basis of poor health or disability. Unlike objectively defined quality of life, everyone has the potential both to enjoy well-being and, crucially for policy, to experience improvements to well-being. Thus well-being can be thought of as an overarching concept, the realisation of which is contingent on people being sufficiently healthy, socially included etc. *for them* to have meaning in life, fulfil their potential and feel that their lives are worthwhile.

This focus on individual subjective experience and meaning fits well with what users of health and social care services in general have said is important to them in life. In a recent interview study with 230 service users who were older, had a learning disability or used mental health services, many individuals with poor health and/or who experienced considerable disability including those with dementia, nonetheless reported being happy with life (Petch *et al.*, 2007). Furthermore, while there was considerable agreement between individuals as to the overarching things that were important in life, e.g. seeing people and having things to do, what this looked like for the different individuals varied enormously. For example, while many people with learning difficulties particularly valued opportunities to socialise with people who did not share their experience of impairment, many people using mental health services preferred spending time with other service users with whom they could be open about their mental health problems. These insights highlight the appropriateness of 'improved well-being' as a goal for policy makers seeking to improve the lives of vulnerable adults.

Well-being for people with dementia

Given the fundamental importance of well-being to people with dementia, it is surprising that a review of the research literature for well-being and dementia generates little material. Instead most researchers working within the field have tended to focus on quality of life, reflecting the dominance of medical and psychological research in this field that has sought to develop objective measures to evaluate the effectiveness of interventions and therapies for dementia. As with the literature on well-being and quality of life more generally, research into dementia, well-being and quality of life is also beset with inconsistencies and contradictions (e.g. Droes *et al.*, 2006). Not only are the terms 'well-being' and 'quality of life' routinely conflated, but a review of nine different quality of life measures found that they differed in relation to the domains of life included and their focus on subjective and objective measures of experience (Ready and Ott, 2003). There is, however, a body of research that has shed light on what well-being means and how it is experienced for people with dementia. This research has predominantly stemmed from the 'social model of dementia', a term used to refer to a range of approaches to understanding dementia that focus on the influence of wider social, cultural, institutional or interpersonal factors on the experience of dementia as opposed to the pathology underlying the condition.

At the centre of the social model of dementia is the recognition that the well-being of people with dementia is contingent on their personhood being supported. 'Personhood' is the term first used by Tom Kitwood in this context to refer to the feeling of still being a person as evidenced by engagement in shared experiences with others (Kitwood, 1987). In the late 1980s and early 1990s Tom Kitwood was one of several researchers who identified the extent to which the personhood, or sense of self, of people with dementia was being unnecessarily undermined as a consequence of the poor care they received. Evaluations of care environments for people with dementia in the early 1980s highlighted the low levels of interaction experienced by individuals living in them (e.g. Godlove *et al.*, 1982; Kitwood, 1987; McCormack and Whitehead, 1981). Previously these low levels of interaction had been attributed to the communicative impairments experienced by people with dementia; however, a few dissenting voices from the field of dementia care challenged these preconceptions. In particular Tom Kitwood (1987; 1997) highlighted the low social status of older people with dementia and the poor quality of the caring environments in which many people with dementia lived. He argued that these poor care environments and the resulting malignant social psychology exacerbated the experiences of confusion and impairment among people with dementia (Kitwood, 1997, p. 45). Thus he argued that the experience of dementia was not solely the result of neuropathology, but was also influenced by psychosocial and environmental factors (Kitwood, 1987; 1997).

These insights led him to develop the person-centred approach to dementia care, which highlighted the need to look beyond dementia and treat every person in care as an individual, responding to their individual needs (Kitwood, 1997). Through this individualised care, he argued, caring environments might support the personhood of people with dementia, the key goal of person-centred care. Communication was highlighted as being central to the maintenance of personhood and well-being, good communication being vital to maintaining personhood while poor communication was identified as threatening the personhood of people with dementia. Kitwood (1997) argued that the application of person-centred care could reduce the malignant social psychology, present in so many care environments for people with dementia, and lead to an improvement in functioning. He termed this 'rementia'. With colleagues in Bradford he devised a tool, Dementia Care Mapping (DCM), to measure the extent to which a person with dementia's personhood was supported by any particular care environment (Bredin *et al.*, 1995) and identified 12 indicators of well-being for people with dementia. These have since been updated by researchers at the Bradford Dementia Group who have developed the well-being profile, a tool to encourage people working in care settings to improve the well-being of individuals and groups of people with dementia (Bruce, 2000). This tool identifies the following 14 indicators of well-being, which state that the person:

- can communicate wants, needs and choices;
- makes contact with other people;
- shows warmth or affection;
- shows pleasure or enjoyment;
- shows alertness and responsiveness;
- uses remaining abilities;
- expresses self-creativity;
- is co-operative and/or helpful;
- responds appropriately to people/situations;
- expresses appropriate emotions;
- has relaxed posture or body language;
- reveals a sense of humour;
- has a sense of purpose;
- shows signs of self-respect.

Researchers working with people with dementia, even in the final stages of the condition, have shown that well-being, as evidenced by these indicators, is entirely possible with good communication and person-centred care. For example, the work of John Killick and Kate Allan has shown that people in the most advanced stages of dementia can make jokes, communicate their intentions, thrive on relationships and social contact with others and be creative, for example by telling stories and making up poems about their lives and their current situation (e.g. Killick and Allan, 2001). These insights have prompted the development of a number of therapeutic approaches to supporting the well-being of people with dementia including using the arts (e.g. Craig, 2004) and movement and music (Palo-Bengtsson and Ekman, 1997).

This growing body of work into the well-being of people with dementia and how it can be supported through good communication and care has also been informed by a number of sociological research studies that have shown that people with dementia in every stage of the condition are not just passive recipients of this care, but have agency and actively work to improve their well-being (e.g. Golander and Raz, 2001; Hubbard *et al.*, 2002b; McColgan, 2001). Ethnographic research in a care home identified three key 'projects' in particular that people with dementia strove towards, through their interactions with others and the world around, that were vital to their achieving well-being (Cook, 2003). These were: a positive self-identity, having social relationships and a sense of self-determinacy. Observations of the older residents with dementia in the care home found that their self-identity, self-determinacy and social relationships were often threatened by the restrictive care provided by the regime of the care home, by their conversations with other residents and staff and also by the meanings they made of themselves in the light of their own awareness of their dementia and frailty. However, the research also found many ways in which both individuals and the care home as a whole acted to support the identity, determinacy of the residents and their social relationships, and that when the older residents had these 'projects' supported they did have well-being.

The importance of self-identity, social relationships and having some control over life to the well-being of people with dementia has been reiterated by the growing body of research that has sought the views of people with dementia directly. As discussed in the previous section, over the past 15 years there has been a significant move within the field of dementia care and research to 'hear the voice' of people with dementia. Thus many researchers, practitioners and policy makers have sought to find out from people with dementia themselves what life is like with dementia and what constitutes a good life. This research has mostly focused on eliciting the views of people in the early stages of the condition though interviews and focus groups with people with dementia (e.g. Bamford and Bruce, 2000; Dabbs, 1999). Some researchers, have, however employed a range of innovative research tools in order to discover the views of people with more advanced dementia and limited communication (see a number of chapters in Wilkinson, 2002). Finally, increasing numbers of people with dementia are speaking out about their own lives (e.g. McKillop, 2002; Robinson, 2002; Sterin, 2002).

This research has shown that whereas for many receiving a diagnosis of dementia is a devastating process that can lead to a wide range of negative emotions (Weaks, 2006), for some people having dementia is not such a big deal, and is just one of many difficult aspects of life to get on with (Hulko, 2008). Hulko carried out in-depth fieldwork with eight older Canadians with dementia and found that while dementia was 'hellish' for the two research participants who were multiply privileged, dementia was much less of an issue for the older people in her study who were poor, or from a minority ethnic background, for whom life in general was more difficult. As one older black man said, 'I pay my bills, what else I gotta do, what other memory do I got to have?' (Hulko, 2008). Although it is clear from this research that having dementia can place huge restrictions on the lives of the individuals affected and their carers, many people with dementia remain able to adapt and continue to engage in both the activities and relationships that have been important to them throughout their lives, thus maintaining well-being (e.g. Clare *et al.*, 2005; Sterin, 2002).

A number of research studies have added to these insights by seeking to identify the *outcomes* that are important to people with dementia. In this context, the term outcome refers to the end result of a service or intervention for the service user or carer, as defined by them. When talking about what is important to them in life, in a number of studies, people with dementia have emphasised the following outcomes:

- having a sense of purpose and role in life, through engagement in meaningful activity such as paid or voluntary work, hobbies, caring for others, work around the home;
- socialising and having close relationships with others;
- maintaining a positive sense of self identity and overcoming the stigma of dementia, disability and ageing;
- feeling included and integrated in local communities and wider society;
- feeling safe and secure, including financially secure;
- maintaining a sense of autonomy;
- staying as well as you can be;
- being free of symptoms and clean and comfortable;
- living in an environment of your choice;
- having a say in and some control over how support is provided to you;

- being listened to, valued and treated with respect. (Bamford and Bruce, 2000; Cook, 2003; Dabbs, 1999; Droes *et al.*, 2006; Gwyther, 1997; Katsuno, 2005)

Bamford and Bruce (2000) highlight that the people with dementia interviewed as part of their study are very much seeking the same outcomes as older people using community care services generally. They do, however, identify three outcomes of particular importance to people with dementia that are not emphasised in the same way by older adults without dementia: positive self-identity, financial security and social integration. This finding reflects both the particular nature of the impairments of dementia and the profound impact that the stigma of dementia can have on individuals living with the condition. This issue is explored in detail in Chapter 5.

Detailed review of this research on the well-being of people with dementia raises two main issues for policy makers seeking to improve the lives of this population. First, it shows that providing care and support to people with dementia is not enough to promote well-being by itself and that it is vital that the services people with dementia receive see them as a person first and seek to deliver individualised, or person-centred, support and care. Second, the literature highlights the agency of people with dementia and the ways in which they actively work to promote their own well-being, even in difficult circumstances. It is vital therefore that policy recognises this agency and actively supports people with dementia in achieving their goals, including their 'projects' of self-identity, self-determinacy and social relationships. In the following section the ways in which policy makers have responded so far to the overall goal of promoting well-being generally and supporting people with dementia specifically are examined in detail.

Promoting well-being through policy

As highlighted in the preface of this book, commitments to improving well-being are at the centre of health policy in both Scotland and England (e.g. Department of Health, 2005a). This focus on well-being, as opposed to just treating ill health and meeting basic care needs, is a relatively recent policy phenomenon and reflects the increased acceptance by policy makers that health is influenced by social and environmental as well as individual factors (Rosenstrom Chang *et al.*, 2006). Whitehead and Dahlgren (1994) identified a range of social and environmental factors that impact on an individual's experience of health, including their social class, local community, employment and education, and highlighted that health is determined by the inter-relationship of all these factors and not just the presence or absence of disease. These analyses have been extended by many researchers who have highlighted how social inequalities are reproduced as health inequalities, arguing that if policy makers want to address population health then they need to address broader social factors such as poverty, housing and access to employment and education (e.g. Shaw *et al.*, 1999). As a consequence, tackling health inequalities is currently high up the policy agenda in both nations (e.g. *Better Health, Better Care,* Scottish Government, 2007; *Our Health, Our Care, Our Say,* Department of Health, 2006).

A further impetus towards a focus on well-being in policy has come from the disability, mental health and older people's rights movements. Academics and activists working within the field of disability and ageing, in particular, have emphasised the extent to which older and disabled people and those with physical and mental health problems are excluded by structures and processes in society that privilege those who are able bodied, well, young and part of the workforce (e.g. Barnes *et al.*, 1999; Hughes, 2002; Oliver, 1990; Phillipson, 1998; Walker, 1981). Those writing from the 'social model of disability' have been particularly influential in calling for policy makers to overcome the barriers to participation in society that people with impairments face and for their right to live a full and active life in their local communities (e.g. Reeve, 2002; Oliver, 1990). Central to this model is the distinction between impairment and disability:

> Impairment is the functional limitation within the individual caused by physical, mental or sensory impairment.
>
> Disability is the loss or limitation of opportunities to take part in normal life of the community on an equal level with others due to physical and social barriers. (Barnes, 1991, p. 2)

Through such a distinction, proponents of the social model of disability challenged the conceptualisation of disability as a 'personal tragedy' requiring sympathy and compensation from society (Reeve, 2002). Instead they called for disability to be defined as social oppression and disabled people to be seen as 'the collective victims of an uncaring or unknowing society, rather than individual victims of circumstance' (Oliver, 1990, p. 2). These analyses brought people with different disabilities together under a common banner and, through an accompanying model of emancipatory action, provided means for disabled people to fight their oppression and change society (Barnes *et al.*, 1999). With respect to policy, this model of emancipatory action called for a shift in the balance of power so that people with disabilities themselves set policy agendas, as well as controlling how their disability was understood by conducting research. While these analyses were initially developed by physically disabled people, more recently the social model of disability has been extended and applied to understand the circumstances of people with learning disabilities, older people and those with mental health problems, including people with dementia (e.g. Gilliard *et al.*, 2005).

These arguments have been influential in changing the ways in which policy is developed, with service users and their carers increasingly involved at every stage of policy development and implementation. For example, in Scotland a dedicated panel of service users and carers has informed both the development and implementation of *Changing Lives: 21st Century Social Work Review* (Scottish Executive, 2006a). Furthermore, the social model of disability and the increased recognition of the rights of service users and their carers to lead a full and active life have led to the development of a more aspirational health and social care policy. For example, the National Service Framework (NSF) for Older People (Department of Health, 2001) includes Standard 8, the promotion of health and an active life in old age.

Hand in hand with this drive towards well-being has been the recognition of the need for statutory agencies to work in partnership to deliver these improvements to the individual's whole life. The NSF for Older People explicitly recognises that partnership working between NHS organisations, local authorities and other agencies is vital to delivering on Standard 8, explicitly making the link between access to community amenities, such as transport links, libraries and leisure facilities and good health in old age. As a result, improving partnership working between health, social care and other statutory, voluntary and private sector agencies is an agenda that has been pursued vigorously by both administrations. In England, the 1999 Health Act (Department of Health, 1999) put in place the legislation to allow pooling of budgets, joint management and commissioning of services. In Scotland, the Joint Future Unit has developed this agenda and formal partnership agreements are now in place between every local authority and health board in Scotland (see Petch, 2007, in this series for a detailed examination of the development and implementation of this agenda).

The emphasis on improving well-being through partnership working is a key characteristic of the drive to modernise public services initiated by the New Labour Government when it came into power in 1997. The White Paper *Modernising Adult Social Care Services* (Department of Health, 1998) outlined a number of initiatives to improve the accountability and efficiency of social care services, both in terms of delivering value for money to the tax payer and delivering well-being for service users and their carers. At the centre of this modernisation agenda has been the development of inspection, regulation and performance management regimes to ensure that all statutorily funded agencies deliver 'best value', including through setting targets to drive change and increase efficiency. This shift in emphasis has led to the identification of a range of outcomes that services should be delivering.

Initially these outcomes related to the process of care and support, for example numbers of assessments carried out, but more recently policy makers have explicitly articulated a range of outcomes for service users and carers that should be achieved as a result of the implementation of specific policies. In this way, policy has sought to keep the well-being of service users and carers at the top of the agenda and ensure that resources are used in ways that benefit the individual, as opposed to just ticking boxes for the organisation. Furthermore, the focus on outcomes has also been used to encourage joint working between agencies. Most recently, health and social care partnerships in Scotland are being encouraged to measure their performance in relation to a range of outcomes for service users and carers as part of the new performance management framework for local authorities, the Single Outcome Agreement.

The outcomes articulated in the prominent policy documents in both England and Scotland are summarised in Table 1.1 and reflect the commitment of recent policy to make a difference to the person's whole life. It

Table 1.1 Summary of service user and carer outcomes articulated within recent health and social care policy

Policy	Outcomes
Putting People First (Department of Health, 2008a)	Live independently Stay healthy and recover quickly Sustain a family unit Maximise control Participate as active and equal citizens economically and socially Best quality of life possible regardless of disability Maintain dignity and respect
Independence, Well-being and Choice (Department of Health, 2005a)	Health Quality of life Positive contribution Choice and control Freedom from discrimination Economic well-being Personal dignity
Changing Lives (Scottish Executive, 2006a)	Personalisation through participation
National Outcomes for Community Care (Joint Future Unit, 2007)	**High Level Outcomes** Improved Well-being Improved Health Improved Social Inclusion Improved Independence and Responsibility **Measures of user and carer outcomes** Feeling safe Satisfied with involvement in package of care (service user and carer) Satisfied with opportunities to engage in social interaction Carer supported and feeling able to continue in their role as carer

is promising that these outcomes overlap considerably with those articulated as important to people with dementia, and include attention not just
to what their life is like, but also to the way in which people are treated by
services, emphasising participation, dignity and respect. Furthermore, the
emphasis on positive contribution, family and inclusion reflects the definition of well-being as articulated by Eckersley (2008). It is beyond the scope
of this book to examine all of the outcomes articulated here. However, in
the following chapters the potential for policy to make a difference to the
well-being of people with dementia will be examined as it relates specifically to four of these outcomes: health, independence, choice and control,
and social inclusion. First, however, the way in which dementia has been
addressed by policy makers to date is discussed.

Dementia in policy

Up until 2007, dementia received very little mention in either mainstream
policy or policies for older people or mental health and while both nations
published guidance on the management and treatment of dementia[1] and
service development[2] there was little in the way of policy with teeth to
drive change. In England, dementia was only included specifically under
one of the seven standards of the *National Service Framework for Older
People* (Department of Health, 2001), the ten-year programme of action to
improve services for and promote independence and health to older people.
Furthermore, dementia was explicitly excluded from the National Framework for Mental Health (Department of Health, 1999), which addressed
mental health services for working age adults. In Scotland, dementia has
been included in key policies designed to improve treatment and support
for older people (*Adding Life to Years* (Scottish Executive, 2002), *Better
Outcomes for Older People* (Scottish Executive, 2005)) and those with
mental health problems (*Delivering for Mental Health* (Scottish Executive, 2006b)), but it has been excluded from the more ambitious policy
agendas seeking to address well-being for these populations. The most
recent policy for older people, *All Our Futures: Planning for a Scotland
with an Ageing Population* (Scottish Executive, 2007), did not mention how
people with dementia could be included in the broad range of initiatives
outlined in the document relating to healthy ageing and social inclusion.
Similarly within the field of mental health, dementia was excluded from
the latest mental health policy, *Towards a Mentally Flourishing Scotland*
(Scottish Government, 2007), a discussion paper on the future of mental
health improvement over the next three years.

   A key reason why policy has tended to ignore dementia is that dementia does not sit easily under either of the two main policy directorates
of which it is currently the responsibility, mental health and older people.

Although dementia is a mental health problem and treatment comes under the auspices of psychiatry and psychology, the experiences of people with dementia are different from those of individuals with mental health problems caused by, for example, schizophrenia. Thus, the terminal trajectory of dementia makes the concept of recovery, at the centre of current mental health policy, problematic. Furthermore, mental health policy and services tend to focus on those under 65, thereby excluding the vast majority of people with dementia. Finally, the prevalence of concurrent physical illness and/or frailty among many people with dementia means that they require considerable support over and above managing their mental health that mental health services are not geared up to provide (Sargeant, 2008).

The reasons for the marginalisation of people with dementia in policy for older people are more subtle as, while 2% of people with dementia are younger and do not fit into older people's services, a significant minority of older people do have dementia, meaning it should be very much a mainstream concern of policy for older people. There has, however, been a distinct trend within the field of ageing away from seeing older people as the dependent recipients of help and care to promoting active ageing (e.g. WHO, 2002). This shift reflects the more general move towards what has been termed a 'post-modern' society in which people from previously marginalized communities have realised new opportunities for engagement and citizenship afforded by consumption and the rise of technologies (Bentz and Shapiro, 1998). While improving opportunities for older people to engage with society is entirely laudable, an unintended consequence of this focus is that those who are frail or have limited resources, including people with dementia, tend to be left behind,.

A second important reason why dementia has tended to be ignored by policy makers is that until recently it was widely thought that there was very little that could be done for people with dementia to improve their well-being. Over the past twenty years the field of dementia has tended to be dominated by medical and scientific perspectives on the condition that have focused on delineating the deficits of dementia, describing how people with dementia differ from the 'normal' population, and searching for treatments and a cure for the condition. While this body of work has been important in advancing understanding and treatments for dementia, an unintended consequence of the dominance of this perspective is that dementia came to be seen as an individual tragedy and the role of broader social and interpersonal processes in shaping the experience of people with dementia was widely ignored. This construction of dementia as a problem of the individual has been widely critiqued for justifying the extremely poor treatment of people with dementia in care settings and the neglect of dementia by policy makers and broader society alike (e.g. Bond, 1992; Clarke, 1999).

Over the course of the past five or six years dementia has, however, steadily risen up the policy agenda. This increase in profile is due in part to the active campaigning of the Alzheimer's Society and Alzheimer Scotland; raised awareness of the increasing prevalence of dementia; and the change in attitudes to dementia, particularly from the medical profession, brought by the rise of the social model of dementia and the development of drugs to treat the condition (Baker, 2004). In 2008 both the Scottish Government and Whitehall have launched, for the first time, programmes of policy relating to dementia. In Scotland this programme comes under the mental health directorate and includes a mixture of activities, some of which were already ongoing and others that have been instigated as a result of the prioritising of dementia. This programme of work includes:

- the introduction of a health board performance management (HEAT) target regarding early diagnosis;
- the development of standards for Integrated Care Pathways for dementia;
- funding for post-diagnostic support pilots;
- the development of a dementia forum;
- better information for carers;
- activities to promote the awareness of dementia;
- funding of an arts programme for people with advanced dementia in hospital;
- funding of a service improvement pilot in one health board area in Scotland (completed in March 2008).

To date, the Scottish Government has pledged £630,000 to this programme to fund the post-diagnostic support work and the arts programme for people with dementia in hospital. This sum equates to approximately £10 for every person with dementia in Scotland, which is a very small capital commitment relative to the overall cost of dementia in Scotland, estimated at between £1.5 and £1.7 billion for 2007 (Alzheimer Scotland, 2007a).

In England the Department of Health has commissioned a panel of experts to develop a National Dementia Strategy, *Transforming the Quality of Dementia Care* (Department of Health, 2008b). The final version of this strategy was launched late in 2008, too late to be included in this book; however the draft strategy launched for consultation in June outlined a programme of work under three streams:

1. Improving awareness of dementia;
2. Improving early detection and intervention; and
3. Improving quality of care.

The draft strategy outlines an extensive programme of work to address these three issues and considers ways in which the required changes can be driven by existing policy levers, such as ongoing initiatives to improve the commissioning of health and social care services. The fact that the draft strategy does not, however, have any resources allocated to it is likely to be a barrier to implementation. Furthermore, it is interesting to note that the strategy is firmly focused on improving care and support and falls short of explicitly striving to improve well-being for people with dementia and their carers. In the following chapters these policies will be examined in more detail alongside more general health and social care policy to determine whether they can make a difference to the well-being of people with dementia and what needs to be in place to ensure that they succeed.

Conclusion

Dementia is a serious condition and one that can have a profound effect on the lives of the individuals concerned as well as impacting on society more generally in terms of the need to provide services and support to this growing population. Given the seriousness and prevalence of this condition it is staggering that policy makers have given so little attention to the needs of people with dementia, particularly in view of the extensive evidence of the poor quality of services that so many people with dementia receive. That dementia has finally arrived at the top of the policy agenda in both Scotland and England is therefore very welcome, if somewhat overdue. If people with dementia are to experience improved well-being and policy makers are to achieve their goals in this respect, it is vital that these programmes of policy deliver to people with dementia. In the following chapters these programmes of policy will be examined in detail, alongside the relevant mainstream health and social care policies, to determine if they will make a difference to the well-being of people with dementia in relation to four key outcomes: health, independence, choice and control, and social inclusion. Chapter 2 presents the first of these analyses and examines the issue of health.

Notes

1. *The Management of Patients with Dementia*, Scottish Intercollegiate Network Guidelines 86 (2006) and *Dementia (guideline 42)*, National Institute of Health and Clinical Excellence / Social Care Institute for Excellence (2006)
2. *HDL 44 Template for Dementia Services* (Scottish Executive, 2004) and *Everybody's Business* (Department of Health / Care Services Improvement Partnership, 2005)

CHAPTER 2

Promoting Health

If health and social care policy makers are to deliver on their commitment to improve well-being for people with dementia, it is vital that they start by ensuring the health of people with dementia. As the discussion of well-being in Chapter 1 highlighted, health by itself does not constitute well-being, rather, good health can be conceptualised as the foundation stone on which well-being is built and as a resource that enables individuals to engage in the activities and relationships that do bring well-being. This analysis is supported by research with people with dementia living in a residential care home. It was found that experiences of pain and disability could have a pervasive impact on an individual's well-being (Cook, 2003). Video-recorded observations of interactions between residents revealed that the older residents' experiences of frailty and physical disability limited not only what they could do every day, but also their perception of what they could achieve, leading many of the older residents to restrict their activities more than was necessary. For example, residents bemoaned the fact that they could no longer walk outside or go to the local shops, activities that other residents were given support to engage in. Furthermore, micro-level analysis of the interactions of the residents with dementia showed that their experiences of pain also impacted on their ability to communicate and engage in activities, with residents being less communicative and engaged when they were displaying non-verbal markers of pain. These findings are supported by a survey of older people with dementia living in residential care in Australia who reported that their quality of life decreased along with their ability to self-care (Moyle et al., 2007).

The relationship between health and dementia is complex and there are four main ways in which having dementia can impact on an individual's health.

1. The cognitive impairments associated with dementia can make engaging in the activities of everyday living that sustain good health more difficult. Thus many people with dementia struggle with cooking, cleaning and ensuring that they have fresh food in the home; they may also be prevented from cooking for fear that they will leave appliances on (Marshall, 1997). Taking exercise can also be a significant problem for people with dementia who may get lost when out of the house and

whose behaviour is frequently pathologised as wandering (Dewing, 2006).

2. Having dementia can make the diagnosis and management of concurrent conditions more difficult. The communication difficulties that many people with dementia experience make it difficult to diagnose illnesses (De Vries, 2003), and the memory problems associated with dementia can make it hard for people to take medications reliably.

3. People with dementia are susceptible to mental health problems and there is a high prevalence of mental ill health among people with dementia. This can occur both as a direct result of the nature of the brain damage, for example giving rise to hallucinations and anxiety, or in response to the psychological and social consequences of living with such a serious and disabling condition (e.g. Burns et al, 1990).

4. When an individual's dementia becomes very advanced it compromises the ability to move, communicate, control the bowel and bladder, regulate temperature and swallow (De Vries, 2003; Post, 2000). Furthermore organ systems, such as the gastrointestinal system can shut down in the process of dying (Post, 2000). These problems are all precursors to the individual's eventual death, which may be from end stage dementia or a concurrent condition (Cox and Cook, 2002).

The way in which these different processes manifest themselves varies enormously between individuals with dementia, who, as a result, differ considerably in relation to their experiences of health. Many people with dementia do enjoy good physical and mental health despite their cognitive impairments and research with people with early to moderate dementia has found that, for many individuals, health is not a big issue (e.g. Bamford and Bruce, 2000; Dabbs,1999). Research into the health status of the population of people with dementia as a whole is limited and it is therefore impossible to determine the extent of health problems among people with dementia. It is clear, however, that disability is prevalent among people with moderate to advanced dementia, with 61% of those living in the community and 95% of those living in institutional care needing support with basic self-care, and 50% of those in the community and 64% of those in institutional care experiencing incontinence (Melzer et al., 2004).

When considering the causes of poor health among people with dementia it is striking that all but the health problems that result from the physical impact of advanced dementia are relatively easy to overcome through good care and support. There is, however, extensive evidence that the current health system is not delivering this support to people with dementia (National Audit Office, 2007). In particular, there are two important areas where the system is failing to deliver: in the diagnosis, treatment and management of dementia itself and in the provision of appropriate care to people with dementia, particularly in health settings. These issues are examined in more detail in the following sections.

Diagnosis, treatment and management of dementia

Policy makers, professionals, advocacy organisations and people with dementia alike have all highlighted the importance of making an early and timely diagnosis of dementia (Department of Health, 2001; Manthorpe *et al.*, 2003; Weaks, 2006; Woods *et al.*, 2003). Research has shown that receiving a diagnosis allows the individual concerned and their family carer to make sense of the changes occurring in their lives and put into place coping mechanisms, such as diaries and other cognitive supports (e.g. Pratt and Wilkinson, 2002; Weaks, 2006). An early diagnosis is also seen as important in enabling treatment and an appropriate package of care to be put into place, avoiding crises and delaying institutionalis-ation (Department of Health, 2001). Furthermore, getting a diagnosis of dementia is fundamental to being able to make choices about the care and support the individual receives both at the present time and in the future (Post, 2000).

The process whereby someone with suspected memory problems should get a diagnosis has been clearly documented within both NICE/ SCIE and SIGN guidelines on dementia (NICE/SCIE, 2006; Scottish Inter-collegiate Network Guidelines, 2006). The GP is the first port of call within this process and when presented with someone with suspected memory problems should run a series of tests to rule out treatable causes of cogni-tive impairment before taking a full history and assessing cognition using a short cognitive assessment. The GP can then refer the individual to special-ist memory assessment services for diagnosis and differential diagnosis. Should the diagnosis of dementia be confirmed, staff can provide appropri-ate information and support and the individual can be assessed for treat-ment using anti-cholinesterase inhibitors and / or non-pharmacological treatment programmes.

Despite the widespread recognition of the benefits of an early diagno-sis, there is extensive evidence that across Europe diagnostic practices for people with dementia are poor (Moïse *et al.*, 2004) with the UK appearing near the bottom of diagnosis performance tables. A Europe-wide survey of practices relating to diagnosis and management showed that in the UK it took on average 32 months for someone to get a diagnosis after first notic-ing the symptoms, which is more than twice as long as it takes in Italy (14 months) or Germany (10 months) (Bond *et al.*, 2005). Furthermore, many people with dementia never get a diagnosis at all. Estimates of the numbers of people who receive a diagnosis vary, with Alzheimer Scotland estimating that 50% of people with dementia in Scotland are told their diagnosis (Alzheimer Scotland, 2007a), compared to the Audit Commission's estimate that only 30% of people with dementia in England receive a diagnosis (National Audit Office, 2007).

Even when individuals with dementia are diagnosed, there is evidence that the diagnosis is not always communicated to them. Some GPs have been found not to tell people with dementia their diagnosis at all and others have been found wanting in terms of the way they share the diagnosis. A survey of GPs in Scotland during the late 1990s found that only 55% of GPs reported that they would tell someone with dementia their diagnosis. When asked which words they used to disclose the diagnosis, the vast majority of the GPs reported using euphemistic words instead of medical terms such as dementia or Alzheimer's disease (Downs et al., 2002). More recently a survey carried out by the National Audit Office found that many GPs did not write to the person confirming their diagnosis or providing additional information about the condition, which is a serious omission when communicating a diagnosis to someone with known memory problems. In addition family carers reported difficulty getting information about diagnosis from GPs, who were concerned about breaching patient confidentiality (National Audit office, 2007).

Review of the research literature in this area identifies a number of barriers to the diagnosis and effective management of dementia. First, many people with dementia either do not recognise the symptoms of dementia, or feel that there is little that can be done to help them and so do not approach their GP for a diagnosis (National Audit Office, 2007). Second, there is an extensive body of evidence that many GPs do not take dementia seriously and do not feel they have adequate skills or training to deal with it (Turner et al., 2004; Vernooji-Dassen et al., 2005). A recent survey found that only 30% of GPs felt that they had the skills and training needed to diagnose and manage dementia and that GPs routinely underestimated the number of patients with dementia that they should expect to find within their practice (National Audit Office, 2007). Until recently it was also the case that many GPs saw no point in taking further action when presented with someone with dementia (Audit Commission, 2000), however Baker (2004) argues that the availability of anti-dementia drugs has made a significant difference in improving the response of GPs to dementia. As a consequence, Alzheimer Scotland (2007a) asserts that in Scotland most people with dementia now receive a diagnosis from an old age psychiatrist, suggesting a high rate of referrals from general practice. This constitutes a significant improvement in recent years as in 1995 research by Holmes et al. found that only 15–20% of people with dementia ever saw a specialist.

Despite the presumed improvement in rates of referral to specialist services, the lack of a clear referral path has been identified as a significant barrier to the effective management of dementia by GPs (National Audit Office, 2007). Knapp *et al.* (2007) identify two main streams of specialist provision for people with dementia: an early intervention stream, and a 'serious mental illness' stream, where people in later stages get support from old age psychiatry and community mental health teams. The location of these services within health and social care organisations varies across the UK. In some areas there are specialist memory services (which are designed to avoid both the stigma of either geriatric medicine or psychiatry), whereas in other localities specialist support is provided by old age psychiatry or through specialist community mental health teams. While NICE guidelines recommend that GPs refer people with mild or questionable dementia to specialist services to confirm diagnosis and also to get a differential diagnosis, the guidelines make no mention of how GPs should manage people who get a diagnosis in the middle stages of dementia and there is nothing mandating them to refer these individuals to specialists. This is concerning given that only those individuals with dementia in contact with a specialist can access drug treatments for the condition.

Relative to other countries in Europe, the UK has very low rates of prescription of anti-dementia drugs (Bond *et al.*, 2005) and these rates are likely to go down in the light of the ruling by NICE that they should only be prescribed on the NHS to people with moderate dementia of the Alzheimer's type (NICE/SCIE, 2006). This decision was reached on the basis of NICE's appraisal of the cost effectiveness of the drugs, and has been widely contested by people with dementia and their advocates who have argued that the drugs for dementia are cost effective when the costs of informal carers are included in the equation. Most recently, Alzheimer Scotland (2006) has published the findings from an audit of 300 people with dementia using anti-cholinesterase inhibitors in Fife, which found that the use of these drugs in the early stage of the condition was cost effective. Specifically, they found that the use of the drugs reduced inpatient admissions and reduced the amount of additional support carers needed, as well as delaying placement in a nursing home. Furthermore, the report argues that the continued prescription of these drugs to the 10,000 people with early stage dementia in Scotland would play a significant part in the government response to its other targets of reducing health inequalities.

In recent years, the issue of drug treatments for dementia and debates about their efficacy, cost effectiveness and suitability for individuals with different types of dementia at different stages of the condition have tended to dominate the field. Furthermore, the role of drug companies in promoting pharmacological responses over non-pharmacological responses to the challenge of supporting people with dementia has been highlighted (Heller and Heller, 2003). As a result, issues about post-diagnostic support for people with dementia have tended to be sidelined. Research with people with dementia and their carers has highlighted, time and time again, the importance of good information, peer support and, in some cases, post-diagnostic counselling in enabling people to come to terms with their diagnosis and to put in place the supports and coping strategies needed to maximise their independence and health (e.g. Clare *et al.*, 2005; Keady and Gilliard, 1999; Pratt and Wikinson, 2003; Weaks, 2006). The NICE and SIGN guidance for dementia both highlight the importance of providing good information to people with dementia and their carers, and state that all individuals should be referred for non-pharmacological interventions where needed. There is, however, evidence that many GPs do not have the information available to give to people with dementia and the provision of post-diagnostic support services and non-pharmacological treatments is very patchy across the UK. Indeed in their response to the Scottish Government's consultation for *Better Health, Better Care*, the 2007 plan for primary care services in Scotland, Alzheimer Scotland identified a serious lack of post-diagnostic support services and argued that in some areas old age psychiatry services cannot afford to buy relevant information materials that have been produced by NHS Health Scotland (Alzheimer Scotland, 2007b).

The effective diagnosis, treatment and management of dementia is clearly fundamental to the improvement of the health of this population. Not only is it essential to ameliorate the symptoms of dementia itself, but it is also vital to ensure that the appropriate supports are put in place to prevent the impairments of dementia impacting on the individual's health more generally. This review of the literature highlights the extent to which the system is failing people with dementia, creating a very significant barrier to their good health. It is heartening therefore that early diagnosis and intervention have been identified as a priority in recent policy in both Scotland and England. The potential for these policies to deliver will be examined later in the chapter. However before that the second key health issue, the provision of appropriate care to people with dementia in health settings, is examined in detail.

Quality of care

While people in the early stages of dementia have emphasised the import-ance of diagnosis and treatment of dementia, many people with dementia are more concerned about their day-to-day health and, in particular, the impact on their life of concurrent illnesses and disabilities (e.g. Dabbs, 1999). As highlighted at the start of this chapter, people with dementia have particular care needs and it is vital that staff both know that the individuals in their care have dementia and are properly trained and supported to meet the additional needs of this population. There is, however, evidence that this kind of care and support is not being provided to people with dementia in mainstream health settings. As discussed above, many people with dementia do not get a formal diagnosis of the condition, and so there is nothing to flag up to care staff that someone might be disorientated or have difficulties with communication or memory when they enter a health setting. Furthermore, professionals within acute care settings are poor at recognising and treating dementia and few people are able to access the liaison psychiatry services that should support this process (National Audit Office, 2007). These findings are concerning given the disorientating nature of acute care settings for people with dementia (Archibald, 2003) and the fact that an individual's experience of confusion is exacerbated when they are in pain (e.g. McClean and Cunningham, 2007).

Research with staff in acute care settings has found that many of them are poorly trained and equipped to meet the needs of people with dementia (National Audit Office, 2007). As a consequence people with dementia are susceptible to malnutrition and dehydration in health care settings where the staff do not appreciate that they need support to eat (Archibald, 2003). Alzheimer Scotland (2007b) also reports instances of people with dementia being catheterised in hospital and leaving hospital incontinent when they were continent before admission. Furthermore, a high prevalence of pain has been found among people with dementia in health care settings who are not able to report pain using the kinds of analogue assessment scales commonly used in hospital and who may not spontaneously report pain themselves, either due to their communication difficulties or because they do not associate reporting pain with getting treatment (e.g. Cook et al., 1999).

The lack of appropriate support for people with dementia in acute care settings has also been found in continuing and long-term care facilities. Continuing care is the term used to describe hospital-based care for people who do not have acute care needs, but who have complex health issues and require the attention of a specialist on a weekly basis (National Audit Office, 2007). This is distinct from long-term care, which provides support for people in the community where they do not need regular specialist input but may need ongoing nursing input or assistance with personal care needs. Although approximately a third of people with dementia live in long-term care settings (Knapp et al., 2007), there is a critical shortage of specialist provision in this sector, with only half as many places registered for people with dementia in care homes as there are individuals with dementia in these settings (National Audit Office, 2007). As a result the quality of care in many long-term care settings is poor (e.g. Ballard et al., 2001) with residents not only having few opportunities to engage in activities and interactions, as highlighted in Chapter 1, but also treated in ways that actively impact on their physical health. For example, McGrath and Jackson (1996) found that 24% of residents in care homes in Glasgow were being treated with anti-psychotic medication and that 88% of these prescriptions were not necessary.

These failures have also been found in NHS continuing care facilities. In response to reports by a whistle blower on abuse of older people with mental health problems, including those with dementia, the Commission for Health Improvement Investigations (2003) conducted a detailed inspection of care on Rowan Ward, a continuing care facility for older people with mental health problems in Manchester. This report identified a catalogue of failings including high levels of unexplained bruising, inadequate management and reporting of incidents and accidents, and patients leaving the ward and putting themselves at risk. It described a culture of care where the personal care needs of the patients were attended to according to the routine, as opposed to the needs of the individual patient. While this case is exceptional, the Care Services Improvement Partnership recognised that many of the issues identified in Rowan Ward are prevalent across the UK (CSIP, 2005). This supposition is supported by a recent spot check survey carried out by the Mental Welfare Commission for Scotland (2006), which found that many long stay wards for people with dementia were disorientating with poor lighting and few visual cues and that few people with dementia had access to activities. Furthermore, some individuals had never left the ward in the two years they had been in care.

Finally, it would seem that the problems health services experience in supporting people with dementia are felt even more acutely when people with dementia at the end of life come into contact with care services. There is evidence that, across the board, the palliative care needs of people with dementia are inadequate and people with dementia may end up moving from home to hospital to home again with their symptoms being poorly managed at the end of life (Cox and Cook, 2002; De Vries, 2003).

This failure of many parts of the health and social care system to provide adequate care and support for people with dementia has consequences not only for the individuals concerned and their carers, but also for the system itself. A recent report found that people with dementia accounted for a high proportion of unscheduled admissions to hospital, many of which were assessed in one health board area as unnecessary (National Audit Office, 2007). Furthermore, there is evidence that people with dementia spent longer in hospital per admission than older patients without dementia (Knapp et al., 2007). All of this has a serious impact on the efforts of the health and social care system to improve efficiency through the setting and meeting of targets, particularly those relating to delayed discharge and unscheduled admissions.

This review of the research into the health problems facing people with dementia raises some very serious issues for health and social care policy that seeks to promote the health of the whole population, including those with dementia. Policy makers are however seeking to tackle these issues through a range of measures, some specific to people with dementia and others targeted at the population as a whole. In the following section these measures are examined in detail and the potential for them to make a difference to the lives of people with dementia is considered. The section starts by examining general policy responses, before going on to look at the policies developed specifically for people with dementia.

Overall policy drivers to improve health

Over the past eight years since devolution there has been some divergence in health policy between England and Scotland and this separation has become more apparent since the election of a Scottish National Party Government in Scotland in 2007. In particular, the two administrations differ in terms of their emphasis on the role of the private sector in the NHS, with the New Labour Government in Westminster seeing competition and contestability as being central to delivering better efficiencies in the health and social care systems (Hudson, 2007). In Scotland, however, this agenda has been clearly rejected and instead Public Health Minister Shona Robison has called for a cooperative NHS, arguing:

> We have set out a plan for a National Health Service based on the values of collaboration and cooperation, not the whims of the market. We affirm a unified structure in which decisions are made in the interests of the people we serve and not by the demands of internal competition. A public service, used by the public, paid for by the public and owned by the public. (Scottish Government, 2007a, p. 2)

Thus the major differences between the administrations are in the areas of how services should be organised, who should provide services and how they should be commissioned and performance managed. Having said this, there is considerable agreement between the key health policy documents in terms of the overall direction of health services, with both governments emphasising the need for health services to shift from providing fragmented and responsive care in hospitals to providing anticipatory, integrated and continuous care in the community (e.g. *Our Health, Our Care, Our Say*, Department of Health, 2006; *Building a Health Service Fit for the Future,* Scottish Executive / NHS Scotland, 2005*).* This shift in focus is clearly potentially very beneficial for people with dementia, who, as we have seen, fare badly in acute care settings. However, in their case study of services in Lincolnshire, the National Audit Office (2007) found a significant minority (16%) of people with dementia in acute hospital services who did not need to be there and who were still in hospital two weeks later. This suggests that in some areas at least, the drive to preventative community-based services is not being effectively realised for people with dementia.

A detailed examination of the key health policy documents for both England and Scotland enables the identification of four key policy agendas that seek to improve the health of the general population, including people with dementia. These are summarised in Box 2.1.

Box 2.1 Policy priorities for improving health in Scotland and England

Shifting the 'balance of care' from hospitals to the community, including through the provision of services in the community and special measures to prevent unscheduled admissions to hospitals and prevent the delayed discharge of individuals in hospital while they wait for an appropriate package of care and support to be put in place in the community.

Improving the *management of long term conditions* through providing anticipatory care (that is before an acute episode) and through working in partnership with patients and providing the information they need to maximise their capacity for 'self-care'.

Improving access to health services with a particular focus on reducing waiting times for hospital procedures to no more than 18 weeks, providing non-urgent specialist interventions within primary care in the community and the extending of primary care services to give patients access in evenings and at weekends. There are distinct differences in terms of the roll-out of these policies between the nations. In England the involvement of private sector providers is seen as being vital to improving access, and private health care companies are now able to tender to provide a range of primary care services. In Scotland this agenda is explicitly rejected and the focus instead is on the rights of patients, who have a tight framework for redress in the case of any complaints or problems, and the reinstatement of universal benefits, in particular free prescriptions and eye tests (Scottish Government, 2007a).

Tackling health inequalities and promoting health through a range of special initiatives including healthy living centres, and keep well projects in Scotland and healthy life check and health supporters in England.

These policy agendas are all potentially very positive for people with dementia. Given the poor experiences of many people with dementia in hospital settings, any policies that enable them to receive appropriate specialist support in familiar and local contexts will have a positive impact on health and well-being. Thus policies that seek to shift the balance of care in this way will have a positive effect on the well-being of people with dementia.

One of the most significant ways in which this agenda has been taken forward is through the development of intermediate care services. Intermediate care services are intensive, individualised packages of care, support and rehabilitation that are provided to older people at a time of crisis either to ensure they do not have to be admitted to hospital or to enable them to leave hospital as soon as they are medically well enough, thereby reducing rates of delayed discharge. There is a growing body of evidence that these initiatives can make a big difference to the lives of older people with complex care needs. However, to date, people with dementia have largely been excluded from these services despite the evidence that they can benefit from programmes of physical re-enablement (Department of Health, 2008b). This is because most services are very time limited, often lasting only 6–12 weeks, and it is difficult to realise benefits for people with dementia within these tight timescales. However, research with older people generally has also shown that where these services are delivered within a fixed timescale the long-term outcomes are not as good as when support is provided more flexibly to meet individuals' changing needs over an extended period (e.g. Petch *et al.*, 2007).

In response to this gap in provision, the Care Services Improvement Partnership has developed and disseminated guidance on the development and commissioning of intermediate care services for older people with mental health problems, including people with dementia (see their website: www.cat.csip.org.uk/index.cfm?pid=11). This guidance builds on research carried out at the University of the West of England and includes a service development checklist and case examples of innovative practice. For example, in Amersham, Buckinghamshire, the Dementia Project was set up in 2003 and is funded by the Primary Care Trust to provide dementia-specific expertise within the mainstream intermediate care service. Dedicated staff within the overall team provide assessment, care management and support to people with dementia as well as giving ongoing training and support to their colleagues in working with people with dementia. As a consequence, the Intermediate Care Team receives around 25 referrals for people with dementia every month from general practitioners and old age psychiatrists.

Initiatives are also in place to encourage GPs and other health and social care professionals to pinpoint those individuals most at risk of admission to hospital so that appropriate preventative supports can be put in place. In Scotland the Information and Statistics Division (ISD) has developed an algorithm (SPARRA) to enable health boards to identify those individuals most at risk of admission to hospital, following the discovery that it is possible to predict 75% of readmissions to hospital on the basis of previous admission. The ISD reports that the take up of this algorithm has been good among health boards and community health partnerships across Scotland. The challenge, however, is to ensure that the information is used to prevent readmission.

In England the introduction of Practice Based Commissioning (PBC) enables groups of GPs to pool resources in order to commission specialist services in the community with the overall objectives of preventing admission to hospital, improving management of long-term conditions and improving choice and access to services. PBC is a route to providing the kinds of tailored support required to make the SPARRA algorithm work for people with dementia. To date the emphasis has been on the potential financial savings of this commissioning model for GPs (Kings Fund, 2007) and it is not clear what, if any, the financial incentives would be for GPs to commission specialist services for people with dementia, since access to specialist care will only increase costs as more people gain entitlements to drug therapies and non-pharmacological interventions. There is, however, one locality where PBC has been used to provide targeted support for people in with dementia, demonstrating the potential for this policy, when implemented well, to make a difference to people with dementia. In South West Staffordshire a group of GP practices have together commissioned a community team to provide a range of preventative and social care services to people with complex health and social care needs including people with dementia (Department of Health, 2007b). This initiative has involved working with local consultants in mental health and geriatrics both to identify people with dementia in need of support and to provide specialist services in primary care settings. In addition the GPs have obtained funding from the Alzheimer Society to purchase premises so that they can meet a local need for day respite services for people with dementia.

Alzheimer Scotland (2007b) has highlighted the relevance of policies designed to improve the management of long-term conditions for people with dementia. They point out, however, that to date very little has been done to deliver this agenda for people with dementia, who, as already discussed, lack the information and access to specialist services needed to improve self-care. Similarly, proposed initiatives in promoting health and tackling health inequalities, while potentially very valuable for addressing exactly the kinds of pervasive difficulties people with dementia have in sustaining health, have completely disregarded this population. Of most concern, however, are the policy proposals relating to improving access to health services, particularly in England. Policies aimed at extending the opening hours of GP surgeries are completely orientated towards meeting the needs of the working population and, although on the surface it would appear that longer opening hours improve care for everyone, in reality this can only be achieved through pooling of resources between practices (and the opening of controversial Poly Clinics in England) and the operation of a shift system for GPs. As a consequence these changes improve speed of access at the expense of consistency of care, which is fundamental to the effective management of people with complex and long-term conditions such as dementia (Weir, 2008). Similarly, the opening up of primary care to private sector providers in England may well deliver faster access and more patient choice, but again at the expense of continuity.

This examination of recent major developments in health policy in both England and Scotland highlights that although the overall direction of policy seems very promising in terms of improving health for people with dementia, it is dependent on local policy implementers thinking 'out of the box' to deliver change. In the following section, dementia-specific policies are examined to determine if they are likely to be more successful in improving the lives of people with dementia.

Dementia-specific policies

Scotland

Given the extensive evidence regarding the poor diagnosis and management of dementia, it is heartening that improving early intervention is at the heart of the policy responses to dementia in both England and Scotland. In Scotland policy makers have sought to improve performance through two key drivers. Most significantly they have introduced a HEAT Target for Health Boards to deliver an improvement of 33% in recognition of patients with dementia by March 2011. This target is supported by the development of a Mental Health Collaborative to drive and support the delivery of HEAT targets relating to mental health generally, as well as £9 million of funding. In addition, they have developed standards for an Integrated Care Pathway (ICP) for dementia. An ICP is a document that outlines the ideal journey through the care system that any one patient should take, including the time taken for different stages of the journey, the information provided, tests conducted and issues discussed (Campbell *et al.*, 1998). Both of these initiatives are in their early stages and it is too soon to know what difference they will make to services on the ground. However, if they are to succeed, it is vital that these programmes of work are closely linked and drive improvements in a coherent fashion. Furthermore it is vital that Health Boards go beyond just recording who has dementia to meet the target and actually deliver improvements in their care.

The development and delivery of additional specialist services would appear to be central to ensuring that the HEAT target and ICP standards do make a difference to the lives of people with dementia. The development of post-diagnostic support services in Tayside shows that this can be achieved with relatively low levels of resources. Here seven Community Psychiatric Nurses have been trained in counselling people with dementia and are given continued support through an action learning set. This work is still in the early stages, but evaluation to date has found that the staff involved feel much better equipped to provide individualised and person-centred care as a result of the training and to look beyond the needs of their own organisation (Weaks, 2008). It is very positive, therefore, that the Scottish Government has allocated £600,000 of funding to improve post-diagnostic support services, though as yet it is not known how this money will be spent.

In addition to these substantial initiatives, the Scottish Government has also committed resources to a number of smaller initiatives, including the training of care staff in the palliative care needs of people with dementia and the development of a good practice database to improve the collection of information on prescriptions for dementia drugs, hospital admissions for people with dementia and national estimates of GP consultations. In response to the Mental Welfare Commission report on the lack of social opportunities for people with dementia in continuing care facilities, the Government has provided funding to Elderflowers, an arts-based organisation who use clowning to promote positive interactions with people with dementia in hospital settings. In addition they are seeking to roll out learning from an action research project carried out by the University of Stirling which sought to identify and implement very practical initiatives to improve dementia care in the Forth Valley area (Dementia Services Development Centre, 2007). For example, to address the problem of poor nutrition in hospital, staff in Forth Valley have implemented a scheme whereby the menu cards of people with dementia in hospital are marked with coloured stickers. The meals for these individuals are then served on coloured trays so whoever is working on the ward at the time is alerted to the fact that the individual concerned needs help to eat.

England

In England improving the health of people with dementia is at the centre of the National Dementia Strategy. This document outlines three programmes of work, all fundamental to addressing the issues described in this chapter. These are considered in turn.

The first strand of the strategy outlines two key measures to improve the awareness and understanding of dementia by members of the general public and also the health and social care workforce. These are the implementation of a public awareness campaign and efforts to mainstream education on dementia as part of professional training for all those who come into contact with people with dementia in a professional capacity. The aims of this programme of work are to help members of the public to recognise the symptoms of dementia and to encourage people to come forward for a diagnosis earlier in the condition; address misunderstandings about dementia and overcome the stigma attached to the condition; and improve awareness among professionals so people with dementia receive appropriate treatment and support.

The public awareness campaign, carried out in collaboration with the Alzheimer Society, started in May 2008 and from its launch achieved a high profile in the media across the UK. This high profile has been helped by the prevalence of debates in the media about aspects of the care and support of older people generally, in particular the quality of care in care homes and who should pay for care (see Chapter 3 for a further discussion). While it is clear that this campaign is raising awareness of dementia, it is too early to know whether it will have an impact on individuals' decisions to seek help in relation to their own memory difficulties. It is vital that actions taken to improve professional training and awareness of dementia build on the impetus created by this campaign so that those coming forward for diagnosis are appropriately supported from the start.

The second part of the strategy outlines measures to improve the early diagnosis of dementia and also the capacity of people with dementia to 'self-care' through the provision of high quality and individually tailored information after diagnosis. Central to this second strand of work is the explicit recommendation that new specialist memory services are commissioned where GPs can refer individuals presenting with memory problems for a rapid specialist assessment and the provision of post-diagnostic support. This recommendation builds on the evaluation of the Croydon Memory service, a one stop shop where people experiencing memory problems can go for a comprehensive assessment and for information and treatment. The memory service is run by a multidisciplinary team including a consultant clinical psychologist, a clinical nurse specialist, a senior care manager, a primary care access social worker, an administrator and an assistant psychologist. A recent evaluation of this team found a 63% increase in the number of new cases of dementia diagnosed as a result of the team, and an increase in the diagnosis of dementia among people from black and minority ethnic backgrounds. In addition, 94% of referrals to the team by GPs and other professionals were found to be appropriate (Banerjee *et al.*, 2007).

The recommendation to increase the provision of specialist services is to be welcomed, though it may be necessary for the government to allocate resources to implementing this recommendation if they are committed to seeing new services across the country, particularly in view of the limited expertise in this area currently available.

A key limitation of this aspect of the strategy, however, is that the specialist services are to focus on diagnosis and post-diagnostic support, instead of providing specialist support to an individual throughout the course of their condition. In order to provide continuity of care for people with dementia, the strategy recommends the development of Dementia Care Advisors, whose role would be to act as a single point of contact for people with dementia, providing advice and signposting them to the appropriate services. However, this arbitrary division of support services into diagnostic and ongoing dementia care goes against the overall drive towards partnership working and creates an unnecessary juncture in the care pathway for people with dementia, who could stay in contact with one specialist team throughout the progression of their condition. This model of an all-encompassing multidisciplinary specialist service has been success-fully developed for mental health services users and people with learning disabilities and has been found to deliver good outcomes for those using the services (e.g. Petch *et al.*, 2007).

The final strand in the strategy makes a number of recommendations for improving the quality of care provided to people with dementia in both hospitals and community settings. Some of these recommendations will be explored in more detail in the following chapter, but those of particular relevance to the health of people with dementia include:

- the appointment of a senior clinician in every hospital respon-sible for ensuring a good service is provided to people with dementia;
- the development of older people's mental health liaison teams for general hospitals to improve assessment and to offer expertise in the care of people with dementia;
- improved access to specialist mental health services (and other health professions) to people with dementia in care homes;
- review of intermediate care services to ensure that they are in-clusive of people with dementia.

These recommendations clearly address the issues raised in this chapter, and are good because they constitute relatively straightforward actions that could make a big difference to the support received by people with dementia. The challenge, however, is ensuring that they are put in place across the country, particularly as they will require a degree of capacity building to ensure that there are appropriately qualified professionals to deliver these services.

Conclusions

The review of research presented in this chapter clearly shows that, to date, people with dementia have been dramatically let down by health services, which fail to provide adequate preventative, primary or specialist care to people with dementia. These failings have had a serious impact on the health and well-being of many people with dementia who are denied the right to even the most basic of treatment and information in the face of a serious, life-limiting condition. While the proposed rafts of dementia policies are likely to go some way to addressing the issue of early detection of dementia, improvements in detection will only lead to improvements in health if services to support the ongoing management and treatment of dementia are also improved. While these services do exist in some areas and there is considerable agreement about what works, access to specialist services is fragmented (Kumpers *et al.*, 2005) with people with dementia coming under the auspices of different departments in different areas. Furthermore the emphasis across the board has been on the detection of dementia, and many services do not go on to provide support throughout the course of the condition. This development is contrary to the aspiration laid out in Action 14 of *Better Outcomes for Older People* (Scottish Executive, 2005), which stated:

> As part of the current developments in mental health services, local partnerships should incorporate joint arrangements and joint services for mental health promotion, early detection and diagnosis, assessment, care and treatment planning and access to specialist services. This should take place whether under the older people's plan, the mental health plan, the older people with mental health needs plan or as a specific dementia services plan.

This document clearly called for the development of specialist services that support the individual throughout the course of their condition and highlighted the need for health and social care services to work together to deliver this specialist, joined-up care. This is an issue that will be examined in more detail in the concluding chapter of this book. First, however, the following chapter considers the issue of promoting independence for people with dementia.

CHAPTER 3

Promoting Independence

Promoting independence for users of health and social care services has been a key goal of health and social care policy for several decades (Wanless, 2006) and is still of central importance. Independence is one of the four high level outcomes in the National Outcomes Framework for Community Care in Scotland (Joint Future Unit, 2007) and is an outcome that has featured prominently in the recent Green and White Papers in England (Department of Health, 2005a; Department of Health, 2006). This chapter examines in detail the issue of supporting the independence of people with dementia. It starts by considering what independence means to people with dementia, then reviews the policy drivers for promoting independence. The chapter then goes on to examine the key issues to be addressed in relation to supporting the independence of people with dementia, before reviewing current and proposed rafts of policy to determine whether they can and will deliver independence for people with dementia.

It is important to consider at the outset what is meant by the term independence, particularly in the light of the slightly different conceptualisations of independence held by policy makers and people with dementia. For policy makers, the term independence is virtually synonymous with staying in one's own home, thus 'living independently' is an explicit goal in *Putting People First* (Department of Health 2008a). Research with older people generally and people with dementia specifically, however, highlights that for them independence is more complex. Fisk and Abbott (1998) interviewed very old people living in different types of accommodation and found that people expressed a range of views on what independence meant, including making one's own decisions, having money, not having to rely on family and friends for help, not being ordered about and told what to do, as well as living in one's own home. Importantly some older people in the study felt ambivalent about independence, highlighting the value of accepting help and also relating being independent to lacking a supportive network of family and friends. Godfrey *et al.* (2004) extend these analyses, arguing that thinking in terms of interdependence is more appropriate for older people experiencing disability and illness for whom total independence is not a realistic goal.

Research among people with dementia has shown that for many individuals there are two key independence issues: a desire to stay in one's home and a fear of becoming a burden on others. Most people with dementia interviewed in research have expressed a preference to stay in their own home, which is identified by people with dementia as vital to their sense of autonomy and also to their self-identity (Bamford and Bruce, 2000; Cook, 2003). Despite recent efforts to improve the quality of care in care homes, and in particular to make them more homely, people with dementia included in research in one care home clearly did not construe their current environment as home and instead used the term 'home' to refer to their previous residences (Cook, 2003). Many people with dementia do, however, recognise the need to balance a desire to stay in their own home with the need to achieve other outcomes (Bamford and Bruce, 2000). Oldman and Quilgars (1999) have critiqued the universal drive towards 'independent living', arguing that older people living alone with inadequate support may experience less independence and well-being than their peers living in residential care. Furthermore, for some individuals moving to a care home is less threatening to their sense of independence than risking becoming a burden on their relatives.

Research with people with dementia in the early stages, in particular, has highlighted the extent to which many individuals resist being cared for and fear the thought of becoming a burden on their family (Clare *et al.*, 2005; Weaks, 2006). This is unsurprising given the extensive evidence that dementia can have a profound impact on close relationships, as the power dynamics and roles within a relationship change and two previously equal partners become the carer and the cared for (e.g. Forbat, 2005). In this way, becoming, and feeling that one has become, a burden can have a profound impact on individual well-being, which is closely tied to social relationships. In addition, Askham *et al.* (2007) have described the way in which the demands placed on carers in their research led not only to considerable stress, but also prompted them to act in ways that undermined the sense of self, and therefore well-being, of the person receiving care, for example by withholding keys and speaking to them in an infantilising way. Thus if policy is to achieve independence for people with dementia it is vital that it not only aspires to keep people at home, but also recognises that they live within a web of relationships that also need to be valued and supported.

Promoting independence: policy imperatives

Promoting independence, in terms of providing the support that enables people to continue living in their own homes, has been a central goal of policy for several decades. A key driver towards promoting independence for service users has been the widespread criticism of institutional care as a form of service provision by academics and activists alike. The institutionalisation of older and disabled people and individuals from other marginal groups has been widely condemned for perpetuating the marginalisation and exclusion they face (e.g. Foucault, 1977; Goffman, 1963; Townsend, 1962). Townsend (1981) argued that the very presence of institutional care settings influences social values and attitudes to the care of older people, making institutionalisation a legitimate option. In this way institutionalisation perpetuates the marginalisation of older people culturally, making it more likely that they will be physically excluded from society. The extent to which a move to an institutional setting exacerbates individual experience of exclusion has been widely reported. Research in residential care settings has found that few residents received regular visits from friends and family (Gubrium, 1975; Peace *et al*, 1997). The remote location of many institutional care settings exacerbates this situation with residents neither able to travel back to their communities by public transport, nor to receive visits from friends and family dependent on public transport (Reed *et al*., 1998). The physical separation of people in institutions not only leads to their individual experience of exclusion, but also renders older and disabled people invisible, perpetuating their marginalised status in society as a whole (Barnes *et al*., 1999).

Critiques of institutionalisation have also highlighted the extent to which institutions are depersonalising and controlling, marginalising the individual wishes, needs and sense of self of the residents (Foucault, 1977; Goffman, 1963; Gubrium, 1975; Paterniti, 2000). Goffman (1963) described the ways in which institutions are self serving, working to the good of the institution as opposed to the people in them. Total institutions, as he termed them, forced staff and inmates into a position of opposition, with both sides defining each other in terms of their institutional meanings, rarely seeing the person behind the institutional role. These findings have been supported by the work of Gubrium (1975), whose ethnography of life in a nursing home for older people highlighted the ways in which the regime depersonalised the residents, defining them by their location and the types of care they required as opposed to who they are. These theoretical findings have been supported by rafts of research critiquing the quality of care provided in many institutional settings (e.g. Kitwood and Bredin, 1992). It is no wonder, therefore, that many older people face the prospect of residential care with fear and dread (Peace and Holland, 2002) and that independence is a key outcome identified as important to the general public when consulted by policy makers.

The second main driver in supporting people to live independently in their own home is cost effectiveness. Knapp *et al*. (2007) estimate that the total cost to society of supporting someone with dementia in a care home is £31,263 a year, compared with £28,527 a year to support someone with severe dementia in the community, making care in the community a significantly cheaper option. Furthermore, the lack of adequate and co-ordinated support for older people with complex needs at home has been identified as the cause of high numbers of unscheduled admissions to hospitals (Information and Statistics Division, 2006). As was discussed in Chapter 2, unscheduled admissions are not only very costly in terms of the service provided, but also cause considerable disruption to the overall health system and prevent hospitals reaching targets for waiting times and delayed discharge. Thus, not only is promoting independence vital to the well-being of the individuals concerned, but it is also a critical issue for the health and social care system more generally.

There is, however, extensive evidence that to date the system is not delivering independence for people with dementia. Not only do one third of people with dementia live in an institutional care setting (Knapp *et al.*, 2007), but of those who live in the community a significant proportion are dependent on unpaid, informal carers for support (Alzheimer Scotland, 2007a). Examination of the literature enables the identification of a number of challenges to improving independence. These include: the nature of the condition; the availability of appropriate community-based support services; and the availability of support for unpaid carers. These issues are examined in detail in the following pages.

Challenges to promoting independence

The nature of dementia

Having dementia constitutes a threat to independence at several levels. In the early stages of the condition individuals may have to give up driving or working (Snyder, 1999), which impacts on their ability to get out and about and also their financial independence. As the condition progresses, individuals often require increasing amounts of support to complete routine tasks such as cooking, cleaning, shopping and paying bills until eventually they need help with personal care, including for some people help with eating and drinking. In these ways people with dementia are similar to many other groups of older and disabled people. There is, however, one important way in which dementia differs from other sources of disability and that has a profound impact on their independence and support needs, and that is the issue of risk.

The disorientation and memory problems associated with dementia mean that people with dementia may do things that carry some risk. Family carers have identified a range of risk issues, including cooking, dealing with heating, managing money, road safety, falling and getting lost (Gilmour *et al.*, 2003). This research has found, however, that many individuals with dementia were reluctant to acknowledge and realistically appraise their ability to continue with day-to-day activities such as cooking and driving and continued to engage in risky behaviours if left unsupervised. As a consequence, family carers spend a significant amount of time supervising the person with dementia both to prevent them from coming to harm and also from engaging in activities that are annoying to the carer, such as rearranging cutlery (Askham *et al.*, 2007). This need to provide supervision as well as support to people with dementia has been identified as a key reason why carers of people with dementia are particularly burdened (NICE / SCIE, 2006), leading Mace and Rabins (2006) to describe the task of a family carer as a '36 hour day'.

The way in which risk is assessed and managed can have a substantial impact on the independence of the individual concerned. There has been a tendency within dementia care to minimise risk by restricting the activities of the individual with dementia at the expense of their autonomy, independence and self-identity (Clarke, 2000). Thus, people with dementia who engage in everyday activities that make life more difficult for carers have been pathologised, for example people with dementia who like to walk are labelled as 'wanderers' and their activities are restricted (Dewing 2006). More recently these restrictive practices have been challenged and the value of supporting positive risk taking has been highlighted. However, Manthorpe (2004) argues for the importance of ongoing discussion around the issues of risk, suggesting that the right of an individual with dementia to take risks needs to be balanced with the risk to family carers, professionals and, in the case of driving, the wider public.

Availability of and access to community-based services

While living with dementia does pose an immediate challenge to one's independence, with appropriate support individuals may, nonetheless, continue to live independent lives in the community throughout the progression of the disease. This is, however, contingent on the availability and provision of appropriate community-based support services, notably day care, domiciliary care and respite services for those individuals with family carers.

Individuals access community-based support following an assessment of their needs, to which everyone is entitled. Following the assessment, a package of care is commissioned and managed, generally by social services, but increasingly by professionals from health and housing too. In some instances the individual service user is given the budget themselves to purchase support from providers of their choice (this issue is examined in detail in the following chapter). This package of care may include nursing care, personal care and also support with domestic tasks and social activities, and should be reviewed every year or whenever an individual's circumstances change. There is, however, considerable evidence that many people do not get access to the support they require (Alzheimer Scotland, 2008; Clough *et al.*, 2007) and recent analyses carried out by Alzheimer Scotland estimated that less than half of those individuals with dementia who needed home care or day care were accessing these services (Alzheimer Scotland, 2007a).

The White Paper *Caring for People* (Department of Health, 1989) outlined the vision for health and social care. One of the fundamental tenets of this vision was that support should be directed to those who needed it most. More recently this principle has been operationalised in England through policies to ensure fair access to care services (e.g. Department of Health, 2001). This policy identified several different categories of assessed need — critical, substantial, moderate or low — and instructed local authorities to focus resources on those with the highest need. However, in many areas constraints on resources mean that only those individuals assessed as having critical need are entitled to a package of support, leaving many people with substantial need to fend for themselves. This policy has left many people unable to access low level support, which older people report as being fundamental to their independence and well-being (Clough *et al.*, 2007). Furthermore, the research by Clough *et al.* (2007) found that the current guidelines regarding eligibility criteria for services inadvertently lead to problems as by only responding to critical or substantial need the system failed to see the person in their entirety and missed the problems caused by lots of different low level needs going unmet, such as shopping, cleaning and managing money.

The consequence of these policies is that patterns of support are shifting. Although overall more hours of domiciliary care are being provided, the support is being directed at fewer individuals, who are receiving intensive packages of support in the community to avoid a move to a care home (Knapp *et al.*, 2007; Moriarty and Webb, 2000). While this is important for preserving the independence of those receiving the support, many others are doing without vital preventative services that enable them to achieve independence as more broadly defined. This not only affects their quality of life and opportunities, but also impacts on their general health making them more vulnerable to crises and admission to hospital. For example, people might get help with dressing and washing, but have to pay to have a light bulb changed or run the risk of falling in the low light. Savings in one area might therefore end up as costs in another (Wanless, 2006).

The way in which support is financed has also led to problems in supporting people's independence. In England, once someone has been assessed as having a need for support, they are means tested and people on moderate incomes or above need to pay for support, though they do get attendance allowance and may get disability living allowance which can be put towards the cost of support. This places two barriers in the way of getting support. Some individuals choose not to pay for the support that they need and others may have difficulties arranging that support, particularly when they lack impartial advice about what is available (Clough *et al.*, 2007). In Scotland the situation is slightly different as personal care is provided free to adults over 65 who are assessed as needing support with tasks such as washing, dressing and food preparation (this is in addition to nursing care, which is provided free across the UK). However a recent review of the policy found that in some areas the demand has resulted in long waits for services and that there are disparities regionally in the definition of personal care, with some but not all people receiving help with food preparation and chiropody (Bell *et al.*, 2007).

Assessment and co-ordination of support services

A further way in which the independence of people with dementia is challenged is through the difficulties some people face with the process of assessment for care services and then the co-ordination of those services. Not only are delays in getting an assessment of need common, but practitioners report lacking the skills needed to capture the information required for a good assessment from people with dementia (Cook *et al.*, 2007). This is concerning, given that Moriarty and Webb (2000) highlight the importance of good interpersonal skills in assessing people with dementia. In addition, people with dementia who have complex needs can be subject to multiple assessments from different professionals and are then required to co-ordinate a complex package of care, including input from health and social care professionals who may not communicate effectively with each other. These tasks can be very onerous for someone with dementia or their carer.

Over the past ten years, however, the drive towards improved partnership working between health and social care has sought to overcome some of these difficulties. One significant development in this area is the Single Shared Assessment, where one health or social care professional makes an assessment of need and then shares this with the relevant other professionals. There is evidence that this policy is working well in some areas and making a difference to the lives of service users (Petch *et al.*, 2007), but progress across the UK as a whole is slow. In Scotland the development of National Minimum Information Standards for Assessment and Review should improve this process.

Quality of domiciliary care services

Good quality, individually tailored domiciliary care services are pivotal to enabling an individual with dementia with support needs to remain in their own home. There is, however, evidence that not only are people unable to access these services, but that when they do the quality of these services is often not good enough. Curtice *et al.* (2002) carried out research into intensive packages of domiciliary support for older people and found that, while providing intensive domiciliary support was an effective way of sustaining people at home, the potential for this service to promote independence was not being maximised as the services had little preventative or rehabilitative focus. Furthermore the older clients interviewed reported a lack of flexibility in terms of tasks that could be carried out, a high turnover of staff, problems accessing help out of hours and the unreliability of many care workers. These findings have been echoed in research just published by Alzheimer Scotland (2008).

One of the key reasons for these failings within the home care system is that domiciliary care services are increasingly being contracted out to private providers who cover specific time slots and tasks, as opposed to being contracted to support an individual (Cobban, 2004). As a result, there is little consistency of care. This impacts on people with dementia most of all (Marshall and Tibbs, 2006) as there is not enough time to build up the relationships required to overcome the communication difficulties of dementia and people with dementia are most vulnerable to the disorientating experience of multiple people entering and leaving the home every day. Furthermore, research with home care workers has found that without specialist training they feel themselves ill-equipped to meet the needs of people with dementia, and they too find the lack of consistency of care a problem (Cobban, 2004).

If policy makers are to promote the independence of people with dementia it is vital that they address these significant issues with home care services. One potential avenue for improving the skills of the home care workforce is through the implementation of the Home Care Practice Licence (Cobban, 2004) The tool has been developed by the Dementia Services Development Centre in Stirling to allow home care workers and all those working in dementia care settings to show that they have the skills and knowledge necessary to carry out these functions. The approach follows a similar model to a UK driving test, involving a written theory test, an observation test and an oral test. Up-to-date information about this tool is available from the University of Stirling Dementia Services Development Centre website (www.dementia.stir.ac.uk/projects.asp).

Availability of support for unpaid carers

The final significant challenge to the independence of people with dementia is the lack of support available for unpaid carers. As highlighted at the start of this chapter, a wish to avoid being a burden on family and friends is a key issue for people with dementia when considering what independence means to them. However family carers provide a significant proportion of care to people with dementia, in some cases more than fifty hours every week (Alzheimer Scotland, 2007a). The Carer's Scotland Manifesto estimates that carers contribute £5.3 billion of care every year yet despite that significant contribution only 1 in 1000 carers have had their needs assessed and tens of thousands of people care without adequate breaks or support. Alzheimer Scotland (2000) found that only 27% of carers of people with dementia get a week's short break in a year. Furthermore, the quality, quantity and nature of respite offered vary around the country and change according to the age of the individual with dementia. As a result some people may lose services when they reach 65, while other become entitled to services that they could not access before that age (Alzheimer Scotland, 2000).

The particular strains associated with caring for someone with dementia have already been discussed. It is no wonder, therefore, that rates of burnout and depression among unpaid carers are high. Papastavrou *et al.* (2007) surveyed carers of people with dementia and found that 68% of carers were highly burdened and 65% had depressive symptoms. Moriarty and Webb (2000) found that carers want a diagnosis and information on prognosis; however, in this study, not all the carers surveyed had even been told the person's diagnosis. Carers lacked knowledge regarding services, in particular home-based support, and had little information about voluntary sector services, even though they had had an assessment from social services.

This review of the issues underpinning the current poor performance of policy in relation to supporting the independence of people with dementia raises broader issues that are currently being debated about the funding and provision of social care for users of health and social care services generally. In the following section we will consider how policy makers have sought to respond to these issues, which affect all users of health and social care services, in order to promote independence for people with dementia.

Promoting the independence of people with dementia: policy responses

Debates about how best to support the independence of users of health and social care services generally as well as people with dementia specifically are currently high on the policy agenda. In particular, debates centre on the levels of support that should be provided to individuals and who should pay for that support. Thus early in 2008 Gordon Brown called for an inquiry into who should pay for social care, in the light of a growing body of evidence that the current system of funding is inequitable, inefficient and disproportionately disadvantages those with middle incomes who have saved for their retirement (e.g. Caring Choices, 2008). These debates have in part been informed by the Wanless report on the future of social care for older people, which was commissioned by the Kings Fund (Wanless, 2006). The report was commissioned in response to increasing concern about the impact of the growing population of older people on the health and social care system, which, it is recognised, does not currently meet the basic needs of this population. The report identified three different scenarios for the future funding of long-term care and projected costs on the basis of continuing to fund social care at current level; funding to what the report referred to as a core business level, i.e. funding to meet basic outcomes, but no more; and finally funding to a level that would actively promote the well-being of older people. The report identified three potential models for future funding: a partnership model whereby care is part funded by the state and part by the individual; free personal care as is currently the model in Scotland; and a limited liability model, where care would initially be means tested and then delivered free after a number of years.

The Wanless report recommends the partnership model as being the most equitable and sustainable model for the funding of long-term care. Further research has confirmed the popularity of this model with the general public, who feel that there should be a level of individual responsibility for paying for care in old age (Caring Choices, 2008). This is despite the evidence that the first five years of free personal care in Scotland have largely been a success, albeit with some issues, as raised earlier in this chapter. These two systems have different merits for people with dementia. Under a system of free personal care, people with dementia do not have to engage in substantial form filling or arrange their own care if they have a private income, and this makes the service substantially more accessible to them. However, as has already been experienced in Scotland, where personal care is free, it is more likely that this system may be subject to rationing, and people with dementia, who may be less able to advocate for themselves, risk missing out on quality support in the community. The more complicated arrangements for financing the partnership model of paying for care as advocated in the Wanless report would undoubtedly prove a barrier to access for some people with dementia. This model, would, however, bring additional income into the social care system from the payments by individuals, thereby potentially reducing the need for rationing and enabling a broader range of needs to be met. Whether this extra funding would be used to provide better services for people with dementia, though, is obviously uncertain.

While debates about the future funding of social care have taken centre stage recently, both administrations have continued to roll out programmes of policy that have a substantial impact on efforts to promote the independence of people with dementia. In the rest of this chapter two sets of policies that have a particular bearing on the independence of people with dementia are discussed: policies to support carers, and telecare initiatives. It is important to note that these initiatives have been developed against the backdrop of the continued commitment to modernise health and social care services, through the improvement of partnership working between health and social care, the opening up of the market to third sector care providers and the development of new ways of commissioning and providing services (which will be discussed in detail in the following chapter).

Supporting carers

Despite the fundamental role of carers in supporting the independence of people with dementia, initiatives to support carers do not feature prominently in the packages of dementia-specific policy launched in either England or Scotland. In Scotland the only specific support to carers proposed is the distribution of 80,000 free copies of the Coping with Dementia Handbook for Carers. In England, the National Dementia Strategy outlines proposals to improve the information provided to carers of people with dementia as part of initiatives to develop better diagnostic and post-diagnostic support services. In addition, the strategy highlights the need for commissioners to ensure the provision of innovative short breaks for people with dementia to enable carers to have a break from caring.

Although none of these initiatives will have much bearing on their own, it is important to note that the dementia-specific policies have been developed in the context of the broader commitment to supporting carers articulated by both administrations. In England, the Government's short- and long-term agenda for carers was laid out in the latest carers strategy, launched in June 2008 (HM Government, 2008). This strategy outlines a number of proposals including improved access to information, training and funding for emergency support for carers, and initiatives to help carers sustain employment, such as flexible working arrangements. This broad view of the role and needs of carers is welcome, as is the commitment of £255 million to underpin the implementation of the strategy in the short term. However, the strategy tends to focus on the needs of working age carers and it is less clear what the strategy will do to alleviate the pressures on those older people providing 50 hours a week or more care for their partner.

In Scotland, one the key ways in which policy makers are seeking to improve services and support for carers is through the development of new Minimum Information Standards for health and social care services that clearly identify carers as partners in care and encourage professionals to support them in that role. Once these standards have been implemented, health and social care services will have to demonstrate that they are gathering information on the needs of carers that should enable them to provide better support. In addition, new approaches to assessing and reviewing the needs of carers are being piloted as part of a larger programme of work on user and carer involvement led by the Joint Improvement Team (Cook *et al.*, 2007). This work has involved the development of a number of assessment and review tools that focus on the outcomes that are important to service users and carers. These tools are currently being piloted around Scotland but early experiences have shown that the focus on outcomes encourages professionals to take an individualised approach to assessment and review. Carers involved in this pilot have reported benefits both in relation to the experience of assessment and the package of care received. However, if these initial benefits are to be realised in terms of improved independence for people with dementia, it is vital that the changes in assessment and review process also lead to changes in the types of services commissioned to ensure that carers are properly supported in their role.

Telecare

The second major policy initiative currently being rolled out in both nations to promote independence of people with dementia specifically and older adults generally is telecare. Telecare describes the range of technical supports provided to people to promote their independence and well-being. Telecare is distinct from telehealth, which is the use of technology to enable the ongoing monitoring of an individual's health at home, for example the blood sugar levels of people with diabetes.

Telecare can include a vast array of technological supports, but the standard package installed in older people's homes in West Lothian, a local authority in Scotland, includes:

- a home alert console, which links sensors to a call centre when they are triggered;
- two infra-red detectors to monitor activity and potential intruders;
- two flood detectors activated by leaking pipes, overflowing baths etc.;
- one heat extreme sensor, sensitive to both high and low temperatures;
- one smoke detector (Bowes and McColgan, 2006, p. 24).

In addition, service users in this local authority may commonly have a pendant alarm to press should they need assistance; a video door entry system; fall detectors; and a passive alarm by the front door to alert the call centre when the door has been opened at certain times of the day, for example at night time.

Telecare was initially developed for people with dementia but is currently being rolled out with much enthusiasm in both England and Scotland for older adults more generally (Woolham et al., 2006). In Scotland, £8 million was pledged to the implementation of telecare as part of the National Telecare Development Programme, and a new strategy has just been published for the mainstreaming of technology needed to run telecare services in every new home in Scotland. In England, the mainstreaming of telecare is a central commitment in the concordat *Putting People First* (Department of Health, 2008a) and the Department of Health has set targets for the local implementation of telecare since 2005 (Woolham *et al.*, (2006).

Research into the use of telecare has shown that it can be an effective and cost-effective means of supporting people at home. Bowes and Mc-Colgan (2006) conducted a three-year evaluation of the implementation of telecare in West Lothian, Scotland, and found that while it took time for people to get used to the technology, when applied in the context of an empowering model of home care, telecare was effective for all but those with the most critical needs. This evaluation found that in general older people, including those with dementia, did not find the technology obtrusive and it helped many of them feel much safer in their own homes and alleviated the stress on carers. Furthermore, several participants described events that would have resulted in serious injury or harm if the telecare system had not been installed and implemented in a timely and person-centred fashion. In addition, economic analyses suggest that the use of telecare in this local authority was cost effective. These findings are supported by statistics on the performance of telecare published by the Scottish Government, who argue that the first stage roll out of telecare in Scotland kept 6000 people at home who wouldn't have stayed without the support, saving £7.1 million (Joint Improvement Team, 2008).

It is clear that the commitment to telecare demonstrated by both administrations has the potential to make a difference to the independence of people with dementia. Lessons from the West Lothian evaluation, however, highlighted the vital importance of technology being delivered as part of an individualised package of care, and used where it is most needed, rather than being provided as a one-size-fits-all model. Furthermore, if the benefits of telecare for people with dementia are to be maximised it is vital that it is rolled out alongside good models of care and support so that technology can empower people with dementia, rather than simply reducing harm.

Conclusions

Promoting the independence of people with dementia is an ambition at the very centre of health and social care policy, not just because that is what people with dementia want, but also because finding a sustainable and affordable solution for supporting all users of health and social care services in their own homes is central to the continued functioning of the health and social care system. This is an issue that in one vital respect the administrations in Scotland and England have approached very differently, with Scotland providing personal care, which is central to the support of independence, free at the point of delivery, whereas in England this support is means tested. However, in other respects the two systems are very similar and are both characterised currently by their failure to adequately meet the needs of people with dementia in their own homes.

While specific initiatives around carers and new technology are important, if policy is to promote the well-being of people with dementia it is vital that it addresses the fundamental gaps in the provision and quality of services to people with dementia in their own homes. The National Dementia Strategy in England highlights the role of new models of commissioning and also the drive towards personalised services in delivering these services. These issues are examined in more detail in the following chapter.

CHAPTER 4

Promoting Choice and Control

Commitments to deliver choice and control to service users and their carers are at the centre of health and social care policy in both Scotland and England and are seen not only as important outcomes in their own right, but also as being fundamental to the broader policy objectives of promoting independence and preventing disability and ill-health (e.g. Glasby and Littlechild, 2006). Morris (2006) argues that having choice and control is essential for self-determination, which she sees as being vital to enabling individuals to realise their full and equal rights as citizens. Furthermore, statements from service users show that where they have choice and control over the support that they receive, it can make a substantial difference to their well-being, by enabling them to pursue the activities and relationships most important to them (e.g. Stewart, 2006).

These findings have been echoed in research with people with dementia. Being in control and having a sense of autonomy were both outcomes identified by Bamford and Bruce (2000) as important to people with dementia, whose stories reflected their desire to get power back from professionals. Similarly, Duncan-Myers and Huebner (2000) found better quality of life among those people with dementia living in care homes who perceived themselves to have more choice over day-to-day activities. These findings are supported by research in a care home, which found that people valued being able to get up when they wanted and to spend their days as they chose (Cook, 2003). In short, having some say over how one lived one's life was found to be fundamental to self-determinacy, which has been identified as central to the well-being of people with dementia.

Examination of the research literature enables the identification of two distinct issues relating to choice and control for people with dementia. First, having some choice and control over how one lives one's life and the support one receives from services is essential to enabling people with dementia to continue to engage in the routines and practices that they have developed over the course of their lives — activities that are vital to their sense of self-identity, self-determinacy and often social relationships (Cook 2003). These routines and practices might include what one eats and watches on television as well as the kinds of activities engaged in. Second, where people with dementia do have to make a significant change to their lives, for example, to accommodate their increasing disability, it is imperative that they are involved in and have some choice and control over that decision-making process.

There is, however, extensive evidence that people with dementia in general are denied choice and control over day-to-day aspects of their life and with respect to decision making more generally. Numerous research studies have highlighted the lack of choice and control that people with dementia have over their daily lives, particularly those living in an institutional care setting (e.g. Gubrium, 1975, Paterniti, 2000.) Thus many people with dementia have no say in when they get up, what they eat, and who they see every day (e.g. Help the Aged, 2006). Similarly Gilliard *et al.* (2005) found that, in the three case studies they carried out, people with dementia living in the community were rarely asked about their own needs, even though they were able to say how they would like their services to be delivered. This lack of choice and control has been identified by Kitwood (1997) as part of the malignant social psychology present in many care settings for people with dementia which, he argued, was fundamental to undermining their well-being.

There is also evidence that people with dementia are excluded from making decisions about broader aspects of their lives. Tyrrell *et al.* (2006) identified five distinct aspects of choice and decision making for people with dementia. These were: the information received; being listened to; having an opportunity to express an opinion; the time allowed to reflect on the decision; and the possibility of changing one's mind. They interviewed people with dementia about the freedom they had experienced to exercise choice in making crucial decisions about accepting help at home, attending day services or entering residential care, and found that people broadly did not feel that they were supported to make a decision in any of these areas. This is in contrast to family carers who more often reported having received good information. Furthermore, the extent to which people with dementia have been denied the opportunity to make decisions about the treatment that they receive, and indeed whether they should participate in research, has been highlighted and the common practice of relying on proxies to give consent for treatment and involvement in research has been criticised (Berghmans and Ter Meulen, 1995; Post, 2000).

Review of the literature enables the identification of a number of different factors that have led to the restrictions on the degree of choice and control that people with dementia have over their lives, as described above. These are diagnosis; the way in which the capacity of people with dementia is constructed; communication issues; and the availability and nature of support services for people with dementia. These factors are examined in detail in the following section. The chapter then goes on to review policy responses to delivering choice and control for people with dementia specifically and users of health and social care services generally.

Barriers and supports to choice and control

Diagnosis and post-diagnostic support

Tyrrell *et al.* (2006) identify provision of information as being central to enabling choice and control. For people with dementia, therefore, knowing their diagnosis, and understanding the condition and the impact it will have on their lives, are fundamental to enabling them to make informed choices about their daily lives and to plan for the future (Post, 2000). An early diagnosis of dementia enables individuals to formally state their wishes for the future in the form of an advanced directive or a living will while they have the capacity to do so (Goldsmith, 1999). In this way individuals with dementia can retain their autonomy even after they have lost awareness or the ability to express their views (Woods and Pratt, 2005). However, as already discussed in Chapter 2, many people with dementia never find out their diagnosis and therefore are denied the information needed to make informed choices and to plan for the future.

Conceptualisations of capacity

A second key factor impacting upon the ability of people with dementia to have a choice and some control over their lives is the way in which the concept of capacity is operationalised for people with dementia. The dominance of a biomedical model of dementia and the resultant focus on their difficulties and deficits, as opposed to abilities, has perpetuated a view of people with dementia as non-persons, lacking a sense of self and insight (see chapters in Hughes *et al.*, 2006, for a discussion). As a result, people with dementia have tended to be written off and assumed not to have the capacity to make decisions for themselves. This has led to the common practice of relying on proxies to make decisions for people with dementia and to give informed consent on their behalf for treatment or participation in research (Woods and Pratt, 2005). However, more recently this notion of capacity has been challenged and research has highlighted the extent to which awareness and insight in dementia is influenced by psychological and social factors as well as cognition (Clare, 2004). Thus capacity is better understood as fluctuating, varying according to circumstance as well as how the individual is feeling on the day.

This more empowering approach to conceptualising capacity has been reinforced through the introduction of legislation that has enshrined the principle that an individual should be assumed to have capacity unless proven otherwise and that recognises the fluctuating nature of capacity. This legislation was introduced initially in Scotland, in the form of the Adults with Incapacity Act (2000), and then in England and Wales with the 2005 Mental Capacity Act. In addition, the legislation has put into place a number of provisions to enable people to have a say over what happens to them should they be incapacitated in the future. An individual can now confer enduring power of attorney to a designated other person, giving them authority to make decisions about a person's welfare, property and finances should they become incapacitated. The power of attorney should act in the person's best interests, taking into consideration their past and current wishes.

As a result of these changes the framework now exists for people with dementia to make choices and have control over decisions affecting their day-to-day lives and life more generally. It is clear from the research reviewed at the start of this chapter that this framework is not being adequately applied. Improving the rate of diagnosis is fundamental to enabling people with dementia to make the most of the opportunities afforded by this legislation to have choice and control (Gilliard *et al.*, 2005); however, these benefits will only be realised if people with dementia also get appropriate information and support. Advocates can play an important role in helping people with dementia take control over their everyday lives, as well as helping them make decisions, such as whether or not to move to a home. For example, in North Lanarkshire the Equals Advocacy Partnership offers one-to-one professional advocacy to people with mental health issues, including dementia, in their own home, at out-reach surgeries, in care homes and in psychiatric in-patient services. The partnership also supports volunteer advocates. Research has shown that those advocating for people with dementia need to adopt a flexible approach to their work and may play a role in discerning what people with dementia want from life, as well as helping them express their wishes, particularly when the capacity of those involved is fluctuating (Cantley and Steven, 2004).

One key area where the situation has advanced in relation to supporting people with dementia to have choice and control is in the area of consenting to take part in research. A central tenet of medical ethics is that all research participants should give written informed consent for participation in the study (Medical Research Council, 2000). Traditionally researchers overcame this problem by obtaining written informed consent from a proxy for the person with dementia. This approach, which has no legal standing, has been widely critiqued for disempowering the person with dementia (e.g. Dewing, 2002). Research with people with dementia has demonstrated that if a research project is explained clearly, many people with dementia can give consent to take part (e.g. Cook, 2002; Mills, 2003). A number of techniques have been described that have been used successfully to make research understandable to people with dementia. These include using everyday language when talking about the research (Reid, 2001); providing easy-to-read consent materials with photographs of the researcher (Allan, 2001); asking about the research in the context of a relationship (Allan, 2001; Dewing, 2002; Reid, 2001); and seeking consent on an ongoing basis

(Dewing, 2002; Hubbard *et al.*, 2002a). The move to seek ongoing consent from people with dementia, termed process consent, has been particularly useful in increasing their inclusion in the research (Dewing, 2002). Process consent does not rely on research participants remembering about the study from one day to the next, and gives them the chance to reassess whether they want to take part in the study, having experienced what that involvement entails (Hubbard *et al.*, 2002a).

These approaches to gaining consent from people with dementia have turned the idea of informed consent on its head and have shown that people with dementia can be supported to make considered decisions about whether or not to participate in research (e.g. Cook, 2002). As a consequence, involving people with dementia in research has become the norm for social scientists working in the field and people with dementia are increasingly playing a leading role in that research. For example, Gloria Sterin, who has dementia, has worked with Phyllis Braudy Harris to research the ways in which people with dementia preserve their sense of self. Sterin and Braudy Harris both interviewed people with dementia and jointly analysed and wrote up the research findings (Braudy Harris and Sterin, 1999). Sterin, a retired academic, has also written in the journal *Dementia* about her experiences of the condition (Sterin, 2002).

Communication

A central barrier to many people with dementia exercising choice and control over their day-to-day lives is the difficulties they experience in communicating. The cognitive impairments associated with dementia can result in a range of communicative difficulties, including flat and shortened speech; confused speech; repetitive questioning; difficulty finding words and names; losing track of speech; inappropriate subject changes; reduced positive emotional expression; faulty linguistic reasoning; and reduced comprehension (Alpert *et al.*, 1990; Bayles and Tomoeda, 1991; Bourgeois, 1991; Magai *et al.*, 1996; Mentis *et al.*, 1995; Quayhagen and Quayhagen, 1996; Whitehouse *et al.*, 1997; Whitehouse, 1999). The communicative difficulties experienced by people with dementia impact on their ability to exert control and communicate their choices in two ways. Not only do their problems in communicating make it more difficult for people with dementia to understand what is being said and to respond appropriately, but there is also extensive evidence that the preconceptions of others about the communicative abilities of people with dementia impacts on their efforts to communicate with them.

The way in which the communication of people with dementia has been understood has largely mirrored understandings of dementia more generally. Much of the early research on this subject stemmed from a biomedical perspective and sought to identify the communicative deficits associated with the condition. This body of research prompted a very pessimistic view of the communicative abilities of people with dementia, leading Bourgeois (1991) to conclude 'by the late stages of the disease, mutism, echolalia and bizarre nonsensical utterances may be the only product of communicative attempts' (p. 831). Examination of communication through a dementia care perspective, however, has led to a more positive perception of the communicative abilities of people with dementia. Research examining communication naturalistically and in detail, adopting a broad understanding of what constituted communication, including non-verbal as well as verbal communicative behaviours, found that people with even very advanced dementia could indeed communicate (Hubbard *et al.*, 2003; Norberg *et al.*, 1986). This research highlighted the importance of context, relationship and appropriate stimuli to invoking communication with people with most advanced dementia and highlighted the heterogeneity of the communicative styles and preferences of people with dementia. Furthermore, the research highlighted the fundamental role of others in supporting interactions with people with dementia (e.g. Athlin and Norberg, 1987) and identified the impact of broader social context on communication (Cook, 2003).

This realisation that communication is possible with people with dementia even in the most advanced stages of the condition has led to the development of a wide range of approaches to supporting people with dementia to express themselves generally and express their views about services specifically. Research has highlighted the value of drawing on a range of different methods to enable people with dementia to express their ideas, including the use of pictures (e.g. Allan, 2001), video (Cook, 2002) and poetry (Killick and Allan, 2001). Furthermore, the central role of front line staff in these endeavours has been highlighted. Allan (2001) piloted a range of different approaches with care staff to encourage them to hear the views of the people with dementia in their care, including during everyday activities, such as bathing and dressing. She found that while many staff were enthusiastic about this model of practice, supporting staff to talk about their activities and learning with each other and become reflective practitioners was fundamental to the success of initiatives. More recently, James McKillop, the Chair of the Scottish Dementia Working Group, who has dementia himself, has, along with Heather Wilkinson, published guidance for researchers seeking to interview people with dementia (Wilkinson and McKillop, 2004). This guidance has been incorporated into two tools developed to support practitioners and commissioners seeking to involve people with dementia in decision making around their individual care and services more generally (Cantley *et al.*, 2005; CSIP, 2007). This issue is considered in more detail later in the chapter.

Inflexibility of services and care regimes

A final way in which the opportunities for people with dementia to have choice and control have been limited is through the restrictive and inflexible nature of services and care regimes. As discussed in the previous chapter, numerous studies have highlighted the extent to which institutional care settings are restrictive and focused on achieving physical care, as opposed to meeting the needs of the individuals who live there. The pattern of provision of day-to-day support for people with dementia in the community may similarly be very restrictive, offering individuals little choice and control. Furthermore, people with dementia often have little choice over the kind of support they need, as many areas provide only standard services designed to meet the needs of the majority of older people with dementia. This situation is particularly detrimental to people with dementia who are younger or from minority ethnic backgrounds as the available services are often particularly inappropriate for their needs (Beattie *et al.*, 2005).

This situation is, however, slowing changing and a growing number of innovative services now provide alternatives to traditional models of day, respite and domiciliary care. These include dementia cafés, where people with dementia and their carers can get together and chat in an informal and non-threatening space; befriending schemes; and innovative models of short breaks during the day and over night. In Scotland, the Falkirk Joint Dementia Initiative has for many years provided a wide range of innovative services that seek to meet the needs of people with dementia in their own homes flexibly and creatively. The Initiative facilitates a mutual support group for people with dementia in a local pub, providing a space for people with dementia and their carers to talk about a range of practical and emotional issues, as well as encouraging them to get out and about into their local communities. Through the 'home from home' service people with dementia are able to access day care in the community, in small groups of 4–6 people, in the homes of local hosts. The sessions run from 10 am – 3 pm and the emphasis of these groups is on supporting people to engage in everyday activities, such as cooking and sitting in the garden, and to remain in contact with their local communities. These services are complemented by a one-to-one support service, which provides support for people with dementia with everyday tasks or opportunities to get out and about.

It is clear that there is the growing expertise needed to overcome the barriers to choice and control for people with dementia discussed in this chapter. The challenge, however, is ensuring that the empowering frameworks outlined in this section are implemented with a wider population of people with dementia. In the following section, key policy responses to this agenda are discussed, and the potential for these policies to make a difference to the well-being of people with dementia is considered.

Delivering choice and control: policy responses

The drive towards delivering choice and control for service users has steadily risen up the policy agenda over the past 20 years. Ensuring that services were flexible and provided a range of options was at the centre of the 1989 White Paper *Caring for People* (Department of Health, 1989). In the late 1990s the Labour Government outlined the 'third way for social care' in the 1998 White Paper *Modernising Adult Social Care Services* (Department of Health, 1998). This document argued that the agency providing care was less important than the quality of the care provided and in so doing opened up the social care market to private and voluntary as well as statutory sector providers (Wanless, 2006). More recently, the Green Paper in England *Independence, Well-being and Choice* (Department of Health, 2005a) firmly placed citizenship and choice at the top of the agenda for social care, and plans for implementing choice and control have been developed in more detail in *Putting People First* (Department of Health, 2008a). In Scotland, 'personalisation through participation' is an outcome at the centre of *Changing Lives: Report of the 21st Century Social Work Review* (Scottish Executive, 2006a).

The choice and control agenda has been developed and implemented in slightly different ways in Scotland and England. In the rest of this chapter these different approaches to promoting choice and control for users of health and social care services generally are examined and their implications for people with dementia discussed.

Comparative perspectives on choice and control

In England the commitment to give service users and carers more choice and control has most recently been laid out in *Putting People First* (Department of Health, 2008a). A number of initiatives are being promoted to deliver on this commitment, the most prominent of which is self-directed support. Self-directed support is the term used to describe a number of different mechanisms that give service users control over the budget allocated to them for support services and enable them to make choices about how that budget is best spent. Self-directed support was originally rolled out in the form of direct payments, which is a payment made directly to the service user following an assessment of their need (Glasby and Littlechild, 2006). Direct payments were developed in response to the demands of disabled people who see them as essential to enabling independent living (Hasler, 2006). The payment received is generally equivalent to the sum that would be spent meeting their need through a standard care package co-ordinated by social services. Individuals in receipt of direct payments are then entitled to spend the money as they choose, for example by directly employing a personal assistant or by purchasing the services that they want from private, voluntary or in some cases statutory sector providers. The many benefits of direct payments to those receiving them have been described elsewhere (see chapters in Leece and Bornat, 2006, and Pearson, 2006, in this series). However, to date the take up of direct payments has been relatively low, particularly for those service users who are not physically disabled. Knapp *et al.* (2007, p. 39) state that currently less than 1% of older people supported by local authorities in England are in receipt of direct payments, relative to 7% of disabled adults.

One of the barriers to the widespread implementation of direct payments is the difficulties or perceived difficulties some groups of service users face in managing the budget (e.g. Ridley and Jones, 2003). In response to this an alternative form of self-directed support, namely individualised budgets, has been piloted in England. Individualised budgets are the pooling of all the support an individual is entitled to, including local authority adult social care budget, community equipment, housing adaptation, housing related support through supporting people, the Independent Living Fund and access to work monies from the Department of Work and Pensions (Knapp *et al.*, 2007, p. 40). While social services hold this budget, the individual is supported to make decisions about how best to spend their money in line with their personal ambitions and aspirations. As yet, individualised budgets are still being piloted and have been offered to few people with dementia; however this situation is expected to change. In the meantime a model of personal budgets is being promoted by the Department of Health (2008a). These are similar to individualised budgets, but include only those resources allocated in respect of social care needs. However, the possibility of rolling out personal or individualised budgets to also pay for health care is currently being explored (Department of Health, 2007a).

There are two main reasons for the enthusiastic commitment of policy makers to models of self-directed support. First, by delivering self-directed support, policy makers are responding directly to the demands of disabled people who have been campaigning for direct payments for many years (Hasler, 2006). Second, models of self-directed support fit with the broader modernisation agenda, particularly the drive to improve efficiency by opening up the market to voluntary and private sector providers, thereby introducing competition and contestability into the system. Several commentators have highlighted the tensions present between these rights-based and neo-liberal imperatives for self-directed support (e.g. Glasby and Littlechild, 2006), and Pearson (2006) argues that concern over the link between self-directed support and the mixed economy of care has been a key factor in the lower take up of direct payments in Scotland than in England.

In Scotland, choice and control is also high on the policy agenda, though here issues around choice and control have been construed primarily in terms of personalisation. Personalisation has been defined as the process of supporting service users either alone or in groups to 'find the right solution for them and to participate in the delivery of a service' (Changing Lives Service Development Group, 2007). While direct payments are available in Scotland, the emphasis has been more on promoting the participation of service users and their carers in decision making about individual packages of care as well as services generally. For example, a panel of service users and carers was convened to inform the development and implementation of Changing Lives (Scottish Executive, 2006a). Furthermore, there has been much less emphasis on the marketisation of care. While the mixed economy of care is explicitly acknowledged as a vital tool in delivering personalisation within social care services (Changing Lives Service Development Group, 2007), as already discussed, expanding the market for health care to private providers has been explicitly rejected by the current Scottish National Party Government. In relation to health, policy makers in Scotland are seeking to deliver personalisation by giving the public a stronger voice in the development of health services through Public Partnership Forums and a Patient Experience Programme (Scottish Government, 2007a). Thus in this context, choice and control is being operationalised primarily at a collective as opposed to an individual level.

Implications for people with dementia

To date, it would appear that the roll out of self-directed support for people with dementia has been slow. Ridley and Jones (2003) carried out pilot research into the use of direct payments for mental health service users in Scotland, including people with dementia, and could not identify any people with dementia actually using direct payments. Nonetheless, the draft National Dementia Strategy (Department of Health, 2008b) identifies the mainstreaming of self-directed support for people with dementia as being central to efforts to improve the quality of care for people with dementia and in particular their opportunities to access specialist and individually tailored support. Sargeant (2008), in a short paper for the Care Services Improvement Partnership, has identified examples where direct payments have been used to support the provision of more innovative forms of short breaks in the community. For example, the Stockton Young Onset Dementia Group gives people with dementia a direct payment to cover their entitlement for respite care and allows them to choose how they take this support over the course of the year, topped up, if applicable, by the Independent Living Fund. Therefore people can use the money to pay for a break in a hotel or a holiday cottage, enabling them to enjoy normal family life for longer. This is a good example of how direct payments can be used to allow control over part of a package of care, without mandating the individual to take responsibility for arranging all of their care.

A potential pitfall of the mainstreaming of self-directed support for all service users, including people with dementia, is that in areas where there is a shortage of trained care staff people with dementia are in danger of finding difficulties in employing people to care for them. This is particularly the case where their packages of care are relatively small and they are looking for assistance with discrete tasks. Furthermore, the successful implementation of the policy will demand that those assessing the needs of people with dementia, and supporting them to make decisions regarding how to spend their budgets, develop the skills needed to work with people with dementia with fluctuating capacity and communication difficulties. A number of tools already exist to support the necessary skill development (e.g, Allan, 2001; CSIP, 2007), but these processes take time and it remains to be seen whether individuals and organisations are willing to devote the time and resources needed to ensure that every person with dementia has choice and control over their lives.

Despite these problems, it is very welcome that this ambitious and potentially empowering agenda is being strongly advocated for people with dementia alongside other populations of service users, at least within the National Dementia Strategy. Self-directed support is an agenda that has the potential to make a big difference to the lives of individuals and groups of people with dementia. This is not something that can necessarily be said for the proposals in Scotland to deliver choice in health services through widespread consultation with service users and the wider public. Early consultation initiatives have focused on issues such as opening times for GP surgeries and it is hard to see how people with dementia will have a voice in such a broad consultation programme.

Conclusions

Improving choice and control for service users and their carers generally, as well as for people with dementia specifically, is an issue currently at the top of the policy agenda, particularly in England. The review of the literature on dementia shows that while people with dementia have been systematically denied choice and control over their lives for many years there is now a radically more empowering framework that can be applied to support them to have a say over their everyday lives. The implementation of this framework will no doubt be supported by the strong messages coming from the National Dementia Strategy about the potential for people with dementia to have choice and control. The challenge is, however, in ensuring that individuals and organisations devote the time needed to support people with dementia to make choices. There is the potential for advocacy services to play an important role in this overall endeavour.

CHAPTER 5

Social Inclusion

Of the four outcomes discussed in this book, social inclusion is probably the outcome of most importance to preserving the well-being of people with dementia. A sense of social inclusion is at the very heart of Eckersley's definition of well-being, 'being at the centre of a web of relationships and activities'. Promoting social inclusion, however, is an outcome that features less prominently in current rafts of health and social care policy than the other three outcomes considered in this book. It is only the National Outcomes Framework for Community Care in Scotland (Joint Future Unit, 2007) that explicitly identifies improved social inclusion as an outcome of central importance to health and social care policy. Outcomes relating to social inclusion are, however, identified in *Independence, Well-being and Choice* (Department of Health, 2005a) and *Putting People First* (Department of Health, 2008a). These include sustaining a family unit; participating as active and equal citizens economically and socially; making a positive contribution; and experiencing freedom from discrimination.

Over the course of this chapter the issue of promoting social inclusion for people with dementia is considered in detail. The chapter starts by defining social inclusion and considering what social inclusion means for people with dementia. The chapter then goes on to review key theoretical understandings of the processes of exclusion operating on people with dementia at both a societal and individual level, before considering how these processes are experienced by people with dementia. Finally the chapter examines key policy responses to promoting the social inclusion of people with dementia and examines the issue of promoting the participation of people with dementia in society.

Definition and meaning

Social inclusion is the opposite process to social exclusion, a process that has received more attention from researchers. Social exclusion has been defined as

> the dynamic process of being shut out, fully or partially, from any of the social, economic, political and cultural systems which determine the social integration of a person in society. Social exclusion may, therefore, be seen as the denial (or non-realisation) of the civil, political and social rights of citizenship.' (Walker, 1997, p. 8)

The term is most commonly used to refer to macro social processes occurring in relation to whole populations. When thinking about the well-being of people with dementia, however, it is also important to focus on the ways in which macro level processes of exclusion are manifest at a micro level, through an individual's everyday interactions with the world. Not only is there extensive evidence that it is the micro level processes of exclusion that have the most profound impact on the well-being of an individual with dementia (as opposed to quality of life, which it can be argued is more determined by macro processes of exclusion), but also the opportunities for policy makers to address macro and micro level processes of exclusion are different. Thus this chapter examines the processes whereby people with dementia are afforded and denied opportunities to:

- participate in activities that are important to them, including work and leisure;
- have a voice in their society and local community;
- have relationships with others.

In addition, the chapter considers the impact of broader processes of social exclusion on individual identity and well-being.

This broad definition of social inclusion fits well with what people with dementia have said is important to them in life. Research with people with dementia has highlighted the vital importance of social relationships to their well-being. Indeed, research designed to measure quality of life among people with dementia found that those people reporting the best quality of life were the individuals who also reported the best relationships with family and friends (Katsuno, 2005; Moyle *et al.* 2007). The benefits of close social relationships to people with dementia are multiple, with people with dementia deriving not only companionship and love from family and friends, but also a sense of safety and support, as this woman with dementia summed up:

> One of the main reasons that I do so well is that I know I have my family behind me … I think that it is important that you know that they are there … then that makes you take a bit of the depression off yourself … that's the way I feel … everyone in my family has been 100 percent supportive … so what else can I ask for. I know that if anything should happen that I would be frightened or anything, all I would have to do is just call. I would hope that anyone who had the same illness has that kind of feeling towards their family. That they know that they are going to get their strong support. (Katsuno, 2005, p. 208)

Furthermore, research with people with dementia living in a care home has found that they can benefit from the sense of security that having close relationships entails, even when they have relatively little face-to-face contact with family members (Cook, 2003).

A second issue identified by people with dementia as vital to their sense of social inclusion is having a role in life and an opportunity to engage in meaningful activity (Bamford and Bruce, 2000; Dabbs, 1999). Research has shown, however, that both of these aspects of life can be threatened by dementia. Bamford and Bruce (2000) highlighted that for many people the onset of dementia and the resulting disability result in some people having to relinquish the roles they had previously held in life, such as that of a carer or provider. Other research, however, has shown the extent to which people with dementia will go to maintain a productive role, even when they move to an institutional care setting. Thus participants with dementia in one research study were found to actively create new roles for themselves in this restrictive setting. For example, one women who identified closely with the 'workers' made fellow residents a cup of tea every afternoon, while another women sought opportunities to clean the home in the mornings and used any tools at her disposal, including incontinence pads (Cook, 2003).

These findings also reveal the importance of meaningful activity to people with dementia. In the case of the two women above, the drive to find something meaningful to do to fill their day was so strong that they created new activities not formally sanctioned or encouraged by the home. Thus occupation in meaningful activity can be seen to be fundamental to self-esteem and well-being. Craig (2004) has stressed the particular value of engaging in creative activities for people with dementia, arguing that such activities can open new doors for people at a time when so many capacities and abilities are being lost. She describes the work she carried out in a ten week placement as an occupational therapist in a hospital ward and how through music, movement and painting she was able to both engage with people with dementia and to spend time with them on an equal footing.

Finally, people with dementia have emphasised the importance of feeling socially integrated. Respondents in Bamford and Bruce's (2000) study spoke of their desire to stay connected to their wider communities and also the benefits of getting involved in other group activities with people with dementia. This research reveals the importance of opportunities for daytime activities for people with dementia, as well as their carers.

Given the importance of being and feeling socially included to well-being, it is concerning that there is extensive evidence that many people with dementia are very socially excluded. As highlighted in Chapter 3, not only do a significant minority of people with dementia live in institutional care settings, and are therefore physically excluded from their local communities and social networks, but many others are isolated at home with little in the way of support to enable them to get out and about. As a consequence, people with dementia have been found to be more socially isolated than older people without dementia (Moriarty and Webb, 2000), who are themselves a very socially isolated group. Furthermore, research in care homes has highlighted the appalling lack of opportunities for residents to engage in meaningful activities (e.g. Ballard *et al.*, 2001) and the paucity of daytime activities provided for people with dementia living in the community has also been reported (Alzheimer Scotland, 2008).

If policy and practice are to overcome the social exclusion that many older people face it is vital that they are grounded in a rigorous understanding of the overarching social processes that lead to the exclusion of people with dementia. In the following section these processes are examined and then the impact on the individual is discussed.

Processes of social exclusion

Despite the prevalence of social exclusion among people with dementia, relatively little attention has been paid to the processes through which people with dementia are excluded from society. Review of a broader body of mainly theoretical research from the field of sociology generally and ageing and disability specifically, does, however, enable two key macro level processes underpinning the exclusion of people with dementia to be elucidated. These are the 'structured dependency' of people with dementia and the dominance of negative cultural discourses around dementia. In addition, the way in which these macro processes of exclusion are reproduced at a micro level through the stigmatisation of people with dementia has also been highlighted. These processes are considered in turn below.

'Structured dependency' of people with dementia

Numerous academics in the field of ageing and disability have described how the complex web of social structures developed by modern society to serve the needs of the population and maintain social order can be seen to meet the needs of the 'ideal' citizen at the cost of 'others' in society, leading to their social exclusion (O'Brien and Penna, 1998). Barnes *et al.* (1999) argued that people with impairments (including older people) are excluded from society by social policies that deny them access to mainstream housing, education, public buildings, transport and employment opportunities. Furthermore, the extent to which capitalist economies, through the development of welfare benefits, have systematically excluded older and disabled people from the labour market, denying them access to equal resources, has been highlighted by those working from a critical gerontological perspective (e.g. Estes, 1979; Walker, 1999). In these ways structures in society have excessively disabled a large population of older and impaired people not only making the experiences of ageing and impairment more problematic for the individuals concerned, but also making them dependent on society to meet their basic needs (Estes, 1979; Oliver, 1990).

A key response to this 'structured dependency' (Townsend, 1981, p. 1) has been to develop extensive industries to assess who is and is not part of 'normal' society and to provide care for those who are excluded (Oliver, 1990). As already discussed in Chapter 4, several researchers have highlighted the extent to which the nature of this provision is influenced by market factors and the drive to make a profit (Estes, 1979; Oliver, 1990). Thus, the response by society to the needs of older and disabled people can be seen to be driven by the industrio-medico complex as opposed to consideration of how their experiences may best be accommodated by society (Estes, 2001). Furthermore, Estes (2001) has stressed the influence of the for-profit sector in determining policy to meet the needs of dependent older people in institutions, as opposed to their own homes, which she argues has played a crucial part in driving the high numbers of people with dementia living in institutional care settings discussed in Chapter 3.

These analyses can be applied to the experiences of people with dementia in several ways. Gubrium (1986) argued that the concept of dementia has been socially constructed through the application of processes such as those described above as a way of explaining away a normal response to ageing in an ageist and disorientating society. This social construction labels dementia as a problem of the individual, justifying their further exclusion from society in institutional care settings, and absolves responsibility for having to do something about the social exclusion of older people more generally. While there is now conclusive evidence that dementia is a problem of the brain, as well as society, these analyses are still relevant for challenging dominant practices relating to people with dementia, such as the immediate presumption that people with dementia lack capacity, discussed in Chapter 4.

Furthermore, thinking about dementia in relation to these processes of structured dependency enables the identification of a range of ways in which people with dementia specifically are excluded by structures that do not take into account their needs. One example of this is the rise of use of the internet for banking and shopping. The increasing use of these new technologies risks perpetuating the social exclusion of people with dementia in several ways. Not only do relatively few people with dementia have access to the technology to bank and shop online, and their cognitive impairments make learning this new skill more difficult, but also people with dementia lose out on the financial incentives for conducting transactions online. Furthermore, they may be less able to access local amenities in familiar ways such as using post offices and shops, as these amenities close around the country to accommodate the changing behaviours of a working population who increasingly demand the ability to shop and manage their money 24 hours a day. In this way, people with dementia can be seen to face a double jeopardy. Not only are they living with an impairment that makes negotiating everyday life more difficult, but with the rise of new media, particularly the internet, social structures are changing rapidly and becoming more and more difficult for older people in general to engage in.

Cultural processes of exclusion

The second macro level process of exclusion identified by sociologists is the exclusion of those identified as 'others' in modern society through the cultural signs, symbols and discourses that serve to legitimise the status of some kinds of people, while delegitimising others (Plummer, 2001). In these ways 'others' are excluded in their day-to-day interactions with the world, through representations and language used in both the public and private sphere. The fear with which modern and post-modern societies look on old age, dementia, disability and death has been widely noted. This fear has led to the exclusion of older, disabled, and dying people from the community as well as from the collective consciousness. Featherstone and Hepworth (1991) describe how negative discourses around the ageing body hide the inner selves of older people, a process that they describe as the 'mask of ageing'. Post (2000) discusses the ways in which the 'hyper-cognitive' nature of society has led to the demonising of dementia, and McColgan et al. (2000) illustrate the ways in which failing cognition was described as a disaster by the press reporting on the death of celebrated author Iris Murdoch from dementia. Moran extends this argument in his review of three narratives of dementia highlighting how the terminal nature of dementia renders it 'unspeakable' (2001, p. 259).

A key response to this fear of ageing, disability and dementia has been the move to focus on 'healthy ageing' and in particular on ways in which older people might help themselves to remain healthy into old age (WHO, 2002). This movement has captured the imagination of gerontologists and policy makers alike, who have explored how older people might maintain health and quality of life into old age through interventions such as exercise (Paulson, 2003), drama groups (Old Spice Drama Group, 2003) and volunteering (Scottish Executive, 2007). Although clearly of great benefit to those who have the resources and health to participate in these activities, the healthy ageing agenda places the responsibility for well-being firmly with the older adult and tends to sideline systemic barriers to good health. Furthermore, as discussed in Chapter 1, little consideration has been given to how those who are very frail, dying or who have conditions not amenable to rehabilitation, such as dementia, can be accommodated in this drive to healthy ageing.

In relation to dementia, these processes have been perpetuated by the dominance of the medical model of dementia and its focus on the limitations of people with the condition as opposed to their abilities. As already highlighted, the medicalisation of dementia has exacerbated the social exclusion of people with dementia by justifying the poor treatment and support that they receive as well as the removal of people with dementia from society through their institutionalisation in care homes.

Research from the field of dementia has shown that these structural and cultural processes of exclusion have had a profound impact on the day-to-day lives of people with dementia, both in terms of the opportunities afforded to them to engage in activities, relationships and to have a role in life and also in relation to their sense of self-identity. One of the key ways in which these macro level processes of exclusion are reproduced at a micro level is through the stigmatisation of people with dementia.

The stigmatisation of people with dementia

Goffman identified stigma as being 'an attribute which is deeply discrediting' (1963, p. 3). He highlighted the relational and contextual nature of the concept, arguing: 'An attribute that stigmatises one type of possessor can confirm the usualness of another and therefore is neither creditable nor discreditable as a thing in itself.' Thus stigma is something borne by people who are identified by others as differentiating from the 'normal'. Central to Goffman's (1963) account of stigma was recognition of the difficulties and uncertainty stigmatised people faced in their interactions with others. He highlighted the difficulties faced on both sides with stigmatised people worrying that every aspect of their behaviour will be misconstrued as being down to the stigmatised quality, and people not possessing the stigma worrying that they were being too demanding or patronising. Goffman argued that stigmatised people gained many benefits from interacting with others who possessed the same stigmatised attribute, in particular where they joined together to represent their concerns to society collectively. However, he also conceded that encountering others with the same stigmatised condition forced people to face their own stigma and therefore could be difficult, in particular for people who acquired the stigmatised condition later in life.

Research with people with dementia has highlighted the extent to which dementia is stigmatised and the pervasive impact that this has on their lives. Indeed Katsuno (2005) identified the stigma of dementia as being one of the most important barriers to quality of life for people with dementia. People with dementia in the early stages of the condition interviewed as part of this study identified a range of ways in which the stigma of dementia impacted on their lives and in particularly on their relationships with others. Thus his participants described working to hide their lack of abilities so as not to seem stupid in front of others, and being treated differently by friends and family when they knew their diagnosis. As one woman said:

When they know you have Alzheimer's they will just kind of ignore you. You are just there and that is it. You can go to a family affair and everybody is kind of gabbing and gabbing and this and that. They leave you alone because they figure you don't know what you're talking about, you don't know what is going on. Oh, I used to hate that. (Katsuno, 2005, p. 206)

The extent to which the stigma of dementia influences the expectations and behaviours of professionals and care staff working with people with dementia has already been discussed and is at the centre of Kitwood's theorising around person-centred care (1997). Thus the low expectations that professionals and care staff have of the potential of people with dementia to engage and have well-being have been found to influence their behaviour and in turn limit the opportunities of people with dementia for inclusion and social interaction. More recently, the impact of negative discourses around dementia on the behaviour of people with dementia themselves has been explored (Cook, 2003). This ethnographic study examined the interactions of the older residents with dementia in a care home and found that their communication was profoundly influenced by the meanings they made of their situation as a frail older person with a memory problem living in a care home. Thus even the residents with more advanced dementia acknowledged the stigmatised nature of their situation and worked to overcome that stigma and present a positive self-identity in the face of overwhelming negative cultural meanings.

Of all the troubled aspects of identity that these residents had to negotiate, the most difficult were the meanings they made of themselves in the light of their memory problems. In general residents adopted two distinct strategies to deal with these threats. First, they would downplay the importance of their memory problems, construing it as a normal part of life in the home. Second, residents would seek to distance themselves from other residents who displayed overtly confused behaviours. As one women with advanced dementia said of a fellow resident: 'Don't talk to her, she is a funny women, she shouts' (Cook, 2003, p. 229). As a result of these strategies there was a lot of conflict between residents who frequently sought to undermine each other in fighting for their place in the 'hierarchy of confusion' present in the care setting. Thus, in seeking to protect their self-identity from the stigma of dementia, residents reproduced processes of social exclusion occurring at a macro level in society in a micro level within the home. Hazan (1994) has described similar processes in an Israeli nursing home, where residents sought to portray themselves as the most independent.

This review of theoretical and empirical research has profound significance for policy and practice seeking to promote the social inclusion and well-being of people with dementia as it clearly shows that policy makers need to act to overcome the structural, cultural and interpersonal barriers to social inclusion for people with dementia. The ways in which policy makers have responded to this challenge are examined in the following section.

Policy responses

In comparison to the rafts of policy that have been developed to support users of health and social care services generally and people with dementia specifically to realise the outcomes examined in the preceding chapters of this book, the issue of social inclusion has received relatively little attention from policy makers. While social inclusion (or outcomes closely related to this process) are highlighted in all the major mainstream health and social care policy documents, the general expectation is that improvements to social inclusion will be realised through the personalisation agenda and additional policies to support independent living, such as telecare. The limitations of policies that seek to keep people with dementia at home at any cost have already been discussed in Chapter 2, and it is important to note that just because someone lives in the community it does not mean that they are socially included.

Health and social care services have an important role to play in ensuring that people with dementia who are unable to get out and about by themselves have the support needed to engage in social relationships and meaningful activity, be this in or out of the home. The implementation of the personalisation agenda in both England and Scotland is seen as being the key way in which policy makers can support people with dementia to continue to engage in relationships, activities and their communities (Department of Health, 2008a; Scottish Executive, 2006a). The potential for models of self-directed support to realise the social inclusion of vulnerable service users by allowing them to determine how and where they access support has already been discussed. In addition, policy makers have sought to promote social inclusion through initiatives to encourage local commissioning of innovative services that provide support to service users in their local communities (e.g. Sargeant, 2008). Commissioning innovative services at a local level is identified as central to realising many of the outcomes in the draft English National Dementia Strategy (Department of Health, 2008b).

The main benefit of this strategy is that it builds on the work already ongoing at a local level in both Scotland and England to develop innovative services for people with dementia that support their inclusion in society. As described in the previous chapter, in the Falkirk area in Scotland people with dementia are already accessing short breaks in the homes of local people in the community. A key limitation of this policy, however, is that only those with assessed needs can access services and therefore have the opportunity to promote their social inclusion through the innovative use of support. As has already been discussed, in many areas of the UK support is only provided to those with critical needs, leaving those with less immediate needs abandoned (Clough *et al.*, 2007). The development of a number of dementia cafés across the UK does have the potential to overcome this gap in provision. Dementia cafés provide an informal place for people with dementia and their carers to meet, share experiences and find out more information about dementia. For example, the Kingston dementia café is open once a month and attendance is free for people with dementia and their carers. Importantly these services are open to anyone and are not restricted to those with assessed needs.

While the provision of opportunities for people with dementia to access support in their local communities is important, it does not by itself overcome the broader cultural processes of exclusion and the resultant stigma associated with dementia. It is positive, therefore, that policy makers in both Scotland and England have committed to taking action to improve the understanding and awareness of dementia through public information campaigns, thereby tackling the stigma associated with the condition. These campaigns have the potential to address the social exclusion of people with dementia in two ways. First, by providing sound information about dementia and helping the public see the individuals behind the disease the campaigns have the potential to play an important role in overcoming the fear and stigma around dementia. Second, if the campaigns are successful in encouraging more people to come forward for an early diagnosis of dementia, then the increased prevalence and visibility of people living with dementia in society will in turn challenge negative discourses around the condition.

The programme of policy outlined above is broadly positive. However it falls far short of being the emancipatory agenda needed to overcome the pervasive impact of the broad social processes of exclusion described in this chapter on the well-being of people with dementia. Recourse to the social model of disability provides a framework for the kinds of actions needed to challenge the disempowering structures and processes prevalent in society and to promote the inclusion of people with dementia. The first step in this framework is to ensure the participation of people with dementia in policy, practice and research that seeks to improve well-being for this population, as well as in social life more generally. As already highlighted in previous chapters of this book, the knowledge and tools needed to work with people with dementia to ensure their participation in every aspect of society already exist. The challenge, therefore, is mainstreaming these approaches to include people with dementia at every stage in the condition in all relevant activities, thereby applying to people with dementia the mantra of the learning disabled people's movement 'Nothing about us without us'. If policy makers are committed to promoting the social inclusion of people with dementia it is vital that they start by involving people with dementia in the development of the awareness campaigns described above.

In Scotland the establishment of the Scottish Dementia Working Group (SDWG) constitutes an important first step to this end. The SDWG is a self-advocacy group established by people with dementia and now run with the support of Alzheimer's Scotland and funding from Comic Relief. The group has a number of branches across the country where members meet regularly to discuss local issues. In addition, members of the group regularly meet with Ministers and MSPs, speak at conferences and events, and sit on national committees and decision-making forums, including the Scottish Dementia Forum, as well as communicating with the press. As a result the SDWG plays an important role in bringing issues for people with dementia to the attention of policy makers and the wider public, as well as directly challenging negative stereotypes about dementia.

Conclusion

Evidence presented over the course of this book has highlighted the extent to which people with dementia are socially excluded, denied opportunities to engage in their local communities, with family and friends and in activities of their choice. The processes of exclusion operating on people with dementia are complex and pervasive and are the result of a range of structural, cultural and interpersonal factors. Furthermore, there is extensive evidence that people with dementia feel this exclusion and the resultant stigma acutely, and that this further impacts on their well-being.

Review of the research presented in this chapter makes it clear that there is no one easy answer to overcoming the social exclusion of all people with dementia. It is however, of vital importance that people with dementia are at the centre of any initiatives that are developed to address their well-being. This issue is examined in more detail in the concluding chapter of the book.

CHAPTER 6

Conclusions and Recommendations

Over the past twenty years there has been a sea change within the field of dementia, so that people with dementia are no longer seen as 'non persons' incapable of well-being, but are recognised as having personhood and agency. Hand in hand with this sea change have come considerable developments in research and practice within the field, and the expertise now exists to ensure the well-being of people with dementia at home or in institutional care settings during every stage of the condition. The philosophy underpinning these developments is encapsulated within the model of person-centred care advocated most prominently by Tom Kitwood and described in Chapter 1. This approach to care highlights the importance of providing individually tailored care and support that sees the person in the context of their personal biography and social relationships and seeks to promote their positive self-identity. Knowing the person and building a good relationship over time is recognised as fundamental to providing person centred care, as is a willingness to see the abilities and personhood of an individual in the face of sometimes severe impairment.

Despite the prominence of these ideas, it is clear from the evidence reviewed during the course of this book that this approach to supporting people with dementia is not being delivered consistently across the UK. Furthermore, it is clear that the well-being of people with dementia is being undermined by the quality of care provided to them at home, in institutional care settings and hospitals, and also through the widespread failure of the health and social care system to provide the specialist services and supports needed to enable the effective diagnosis, treatment and management of dementia. Thus, people with dementia are not being supported to realise four outcomes that are essential to well-being and that are prioritised by health and social care policy makers and people with dementia alike: health, independence, choice and control, and social inclusion.

In the preceding chapters, many specific challenges and opportunities in delivering on these outcomes have been reviewed, not least the development of new rafts of dementia-specific policy in both England and Scotland. It is, however, possible to discern some overarching themes running through these chapters and these are examined below.

Challenges

Possibly the biggest challenge to promoting the well-being of people with dementia is overcoming the dominance of the medical model of dementia that has perpetuated the view that well-being is impossible, and justified the continued existence of grossly inadequate care services. Thus, the current administrations have inherited a system of care for people with dementia that is underfunded, neglected and very limited in its ambitions. This poses a considerable challenge for current policy makers who need not only to drag current care and support into the 21st century, but also to plan ahead to ensure that the system will meet the needs of the growing population of people with dementia predicted for the future. This challenge is explicitly recognised in the English National Dementia Strategy (Department of Health, 2008b), which suggests that the capacity of the system should be built up over the course of five years. The draft strategy also highlights the need to raise awareness of the potential of people with dementia to live a good quality of life. However it falls short of either aspiring, or committing, to deliver well-being or quality of life for people with dementia itself. Thus, out of the numerous outcomes articulated in the draft strategy, none relates specifically to outcomes for service users or their carers.

In the current policy context where every new policy document is littered with mission statements, visions and commitments centring on improving outcomes for service users and their carers, this is an important omission. While it is reasonable to question the extent to which some of these statements move beyond rhetoric and into meaningful plans of action, the absence of such commitments for people with dementia reinforces the view of dementia as a problem of the individual for which there is nothing that policy specifically or society more generally can do. Indeed, consideration of the way in which services and supports for people with learning difficulties have been transformed in the wake of two visionary and service user-led policy documents (*Valuing People* (Department of Health, 2001) and *The Same As You* (Scottish Executive, 2002)) highlights the power of rhetoric in the current policy context and the vital importance of involving people with dementia in the development and implementation of policy.

The second overarching barrier to improving well-being for people with dementia is overcoming the pervasive view that this is not a priority. In Chapter 5 the extent to which people with dementia are marginalized and excluded by a culture that fears ageing, death, disability and decline was highlighted. As a result policy makers specifically and the public more generally have sat by for many years doing little in response to numerous reports documenting the abuse and neglect of people with dementia. These dominant discourses around dementia have developed over the course of decades, if not centuries, and are manifest (albeit in different ways) around the world. Overcoming the public antipathy towards dementia will take time and will require some radical action, over and above the implementation of public awareness campaigns. The experiences of the disability rights movement show that if public opinion is to change then people with dementia themselves must be at the centre of efforts to change public perceptions. Policy makers have a significant role to play in this by ensuring that people with dementia are included in the design and implementation of policy and that even the most aspirational policy is inclusive to people with dementia.

The third and related challenge to improving the well-being of people with dementia is the prevalence of negative stereotypes around dementia. As has been argued in several sections of this book, negative attitudes to dementia impact on the well-being of individuals with the condition in two ways. First, the stigma of dementia leads others to act in ways towards people with dementia that are disempowering, disabling or hurtful. Second, there is evidence that people with dementia internalise the negative meanings around dementia, which can be a profound threat to their self identity and well-being. Again, changing public perceptions of dementia is fundamental to overcoming this challenge.

The final challenge to the well-being of people with dementia comes from the health and social care system itself. As discussed over the course of the book, drives to modernise the health and social care system have led to a number of initiatives to deliver cost efficiencies and choice at the expense of relationships between service users and professionals and consistency of care. Given all that is known about the importance of relationships and consistency to delivering quality care and support to people with dementia, these moves are potentially very damaging. It is vital that mechanisms are put in place to safeguard people with dementia from the worst excesses of these policies, otherwise the benefits of the good dementia-specific initiatives proposed to ensure consistency of care in dementia services will be lost.

Possibilities

While there are clearly significant challenges to be overcome if policy is to improve the well-being of people with dementia, over the course of this book some important opportunities for improving well-being have also been identified. The most important of these is, arguably, the very presence of high profile policy around dementia in both England and Scotland. Not only will many of these policies have a direct bearing on the lives of people with dementia, but the existence of these policies is vital in raising the profile of dementia. In particular, the more people with dementia there are who are diagnosed early in the condition, the more people there are to speak up for the rights of people with dementia and to challenge negative stereotypes both in the context of their day-to-day lives and relationships and in society more generally. Thus commitments to improve rates of diagnosis and early intervention for people with dementia are absolutely fundamental to improving both individual well-being and the well-being of the population of people with dementia more generally.

In addition, there are two key features of the drive to modernise health and social care services that have the potential to have a profoundly positive impact on the well-being of people with dementia. As highlighted in Chapter 1, health and social care organisations are increasingly mandated to work in partnership with each other as well as with other statutory, private and voluntary sector agencies. There is evidence that in some areas partnership working is making a difference to the lives of service users and carers by enabling the provision of packages of support that are joined up, address the person's whole needs (as opposed to just health or social care needs), are easily accessible and promote consistency of care. Thus the framework exists for the development of joined-up, specialist services to support people with dementia throughout the progression of their condition. Furthermore, there exist a number of drivers within both rafts of dementia-specific policy to encourage this to happen.

The second possibility for the promotion of the well-being of people with dementia provided by the modernisation of health and social care services is the focus on personalisation. Although a somewhat nebulous agenda encapsulating a wide range of activities from user involvement to self-directed support, the principle behind these policies respects the agency of people with dementia and recognises them as the experts in how best to improve their well-being. As described in Chapter 4, there are a few examples of direct payments being used to enable people with dementia to take control of their lives, for example by accessing tailor-made holidays. It could be argued that the drive to personalisation is the area of policy that has the most potential to deliver well-being to people with dementia as defined by Eckersley. As discussed in Chapter 4, however, this agenda should be approached with considerable caution, as people with dementia are not likely to be well served in a system that is vulnerable to the whims of the market in terms of supply and demand of care services.

The challenge, therefore, is for policy makers is to ensure that these significant opportunities to improve the well-being of people with dementia are realised through their implementation. The review of health and social care policy in both England and Scotland presented in this book has revealed the sheer volume of targets, toolkits, strategies and initiatives that have been put in place to drive change. The proliferation of these measures and initiatives is in danger of swamping those responsible for implementing policy at a local level. Thus, there is a danger of people responding to the immediate imperative of the target or initiative as opposed to responding to the overarching issues underpinning that target as manifested in their local area. People with dementia, who currently have little voice in the policy making or implementation processes, are very vulnerable to being forgotten about in this situation, particularly when their needs are competing against those of more vocal or prominent groups of service users.

Recommendations

Over the past couple of years several high profile reports have been published on dementia, all of which make numerous and very worthy recommendations for the future policy, practice and research in the field (Alzheimer Scotland, 2007a; Department of Health, 2008b; National Audit Office, 2007; Knapp *et al.*, 2007). It is not the intention of this book to repeat these arguments and recommendations; however, analysis of the key policies presented in this book in relation to theoretical and empirical understandings of the experience of dementia does point to two overarching recommendations for policy makers seeking to promote the well-being of people with dementia.

First, it is imperative that all mainstream health and social care policy is inclusive of people with dementia. Given the widespread recognition of the specific problems people with dementia face accessing services specifically and aspects of social life more generally, it should not be possible to publish a major policy document without making explicit how the proposals will be implemented for people with dementia and other groups of people with disabilities or complex health needs. Therefore a key recommendation of this book is that all new policies are subject to an audit of their potential to be realised for people with dementia and that this audit should be published alongside a short guide to implementing the proposed initiatives for people with dementia. The introduction of such a system would ensure that policy makers and politicians think seriously about the consequences of their actions for those who are most vulnerable in society. Furthermore, the implementation of this kind of system would not only benefit people with dementia, but also those from other vulnerable groups who are currently excluded from mainstream policy agendas because of illness, disability or social exclusion. The Alzheimer's societies in Scotland and England could usefully be employed to carry out these audits, or policy makers could draw on the expertise within the network of Dementia Services Development Centres.

Second, it is vital that efforts to support the participation of people with dementia in policy, practice and research, as well as in society more generally are redoubled.

Central to this is the development of a stronger self-advocacy movement for people with dementia. The rise of the disabled people's movement has shown how self-advocacy can make a difference to policies and procedures at a local and national level and it is vital that this model is replicated for people with dementia. This would have the benefit also of challenging stereotypes around dementia and help to overcome the stigma that so many individuals experience so acutely. Again, building close partnerships with the Alzheimer's societies and the Dementia Services Development Centres is vital to achieving this end.

Concluding comment

For too long, people with dementia have been stuck in a spiral of social exclusion. Denied the right to a diagnosis, treatment and adequate support, they have been unable to fight for their rights or to challenge the negative preconceptions surrounding their experiences. The onus is on policy makers, practitioners, researchers and all those involved with people with dementia to support people with dementia individually and collectively to turn this spiral of exclusion around. Over the course of this book many strategies have been identified to improve the lives of people with dementia: putting them into practice is vital for the health and well-being of people with dementia specifically and the health and social care system in its entirety.

References

Allan, K. (2001) *Communication and Consultation: Exploring ways for staff to involve people with dementia in developing services*, Joseph Rowntree Foundation, Bristol: Policy Press

Alpert, M. *et al.* (1990) 'Interpersonal communication in the context of dementia', *Journal of Communication Disorders*, Vol. 23, Nos. 4–5, pp. 337–46

Alzheimer Scotland (2000) *Planning Signposts for Dementia Care Services*, Edinburgh: Alzheimer Scotland

Alzheimer Scotland (2006) 'A Scottish way forward for drug treatments in early Alzheimer's disease', Edinburgh: Alzheimer Scotland. Available from URL: www.alzscot.org/pages/policy/scottishwayforward.htm (accessed 22 June 2008)

Alzheimer Scotland (2007a) *The Dementia Epidemic – Where Scotland is now and the challenge ahead*, Edinburgh: Alzheimer Scotland

Alzheimer Scotland (2007b) *Better Health, Better Care Response*, Edinburgh: Alzheimer Scotland

Alzheimer Scotland (2008) *Meeting our needs? – The level and quality of dementia support services in Scotland*, Edinburgh: Alzheimer Scotland

Archibald, C. (2003) *People with Dementia in Acute Hospitals: A practice guide for registered nurses*, Stirling: Dementia Services Development Centre, University of Stirling

Askham, J. *et al.* (2007) 'Care at home for people with dementia: as in a total institution?', *Ageing and Society*, Vol. 27, No. 1, pp. 3–24

Athlin, E. and Norberg, A. (1987) 'Interaction between the severely demented patient and his caregiver during feeding', *Scandinavian Journal of Caring Sciences*, Vol.1, pp. 117–23

Audit Commission (2000) *Forget Me Not*, London: TSO

Baker, A. (2004) 'The direction of mental health care for the elderly', *Postgraduate Medical Journal*, Vol. 80, pp.187–9

Ballard, C. *et al.* (2001) 'Quality of care in private sector and NHS facilities for people with dementia: cross sectional survey', *British Medical Journal*, Vol. 323, pp. 426–7

Bamford, C. and Bruce, E. (2000) 'Defining the outcomes of community care: the perspectives of older people with dementia and their carers', *Ageing and Society*, Vol. 20, pp. 543–70

Banerjee, S. *et al.* (2007) 'Improving the quality of care for mild to moderate dementia: an evaluation of the Croydon Memory Service Model', *International Journal of Geriatric Psychiatry*, Vol. 22, No. 8, pp. 782–8

Barnes, C. (1991) *Disabled People in Britain and Discrimination*, London: Hurst and Co.

Barnes, C., Mercer, G. and Shakespeare, T. (1999) *Exploring Disability: A sociological introduction*, Cambridge: Polity Press

Bayles, K. A. and Tomoeda, C. K. (1991) 'Caregiver reports of prevalence and appearance order of linguistic symptoms in Alzheimer's Patients', *Gerontologist*, Vol. 31, No. 2, pp. 210–16

Beattie, A. *et al.* (2005) 'They don't quite fit the way we organize our services – Results from a UK Field Study of Marginalised Groups in Dementia Care', *Disability and*

Society, Vol. 20, No. 1, pp. 67–80

Bell, D. N. F., Bowes, A. and Dawson, A. (2007) *Free Personal care – Recent developments*, York: Joseph Rowntree Foundation

Bentz, V. M. and Shapiro, J. J. (1998) *Mindful Inquiry in Social Research*, Thousand Oaks, California: Sage

Berghmans, R. L. P. and Ter Meulen, R. H. J. (1995) 'Ethical Issues in research with dementia patients', *International Journal of Geriatric Psychiatry*, Vol. 10, pp. 647–51

Bond, J. (1992) 'The medicalization of dementia', *Journal of Aging Studies*, Vol. 6, No. 4, pp. 397–403

Bond, J. *et al.* (2005) 'Inequalities in dementia care across Europe: key findings of the Facing Dementia Survey', *International Journal of Clinical Practice*, Vol. 59, Suppl. 146, pp. 8–14

Bourgeois, M. S. (1991) 'Communication treatment for adults with dementia', *Journal of Speech and Hearing Research*, Vol. 34, pp. 831–44

Bowes, A. and McColgan, G. (2006) *Smart Technology and Community Care for Older People: Innovation in West Lothian, Scotland*, Edinburgh: Age Concern Scotland

Braudy Harris, P. and Sterin, G. (1999) 'Insider's perspective: defining and preserving the self of dementia', *Journal of Mental Health and Aging*, Vol. 5, No. 3, pp. 241–56

Bredin, K., Kitwood, T. and Wattis, J. (1995) 'Decline in quality of life for patients with severe dementia following a ward merger', *International Journal of Geriatric Psychiatry*, Vol. 10, pp. 967–73

Brooker, D. (2007) *Person-centred Dementia Care: Making Services Better*, London: Jessica Kingsley

Bruce, E. (2000) 'Looking after well-being: a tool for evaluation', *Journal of Dementia Care*, Nov/Dec, pp. 25–7

Burns, A. *et al.* (1990) 'Psychiatric phenomena in Alzheimer's Disease, III: Disorders of mood', *British Journal of Psychiatry*, Vol. 157, pp. 81–7

Campbell, H. *et al.* (1998) 'Integrated care pathways', *British Medical Journal*, Vol. 316, pp. 133–7

Cantley, C. and Bowes, A. (2004) 'Dementia and social inclusion: the way forward', in Innes, A., Archibald, C. and Murphy, C. (eds) (2004) *Dementia and Social Inclusion*, London: Jessica Kingsley

Cantley, C. and Steven, K. (2004) 'Feeling the way: understanding how advocates work with people with dementia', *Dementia*, Vol. 3, No. 2, pp.127–43

Cantley, C., Woodhouse, J. and Smith, M. (2005) *Listen to Us: Involving people with dementia in planning and developing services*, Newcastle: Dementia North

Care Services Improvement Partnership (CSIP) (2005) *Moving on: Key Learning from Rowan Ward*, London: Department of Health

Care Services Improvement Partnership (2007) *Strengthening the Involvement of People with Dementia*: Care Services Improvement Partnership

Caring Choices (2008) *The Future of Care Funding: Time for a change*, London: Kings Fund

Changing Lives Service Development Group (2007) *Personalisation: A discussion document*, Edinburgh: Scottish Executive

Clare, L. (2004) 'The construction of awareness in early-stage Alzheimer's disease', *British Journal of Clinical Psychology*, Vol. 43, pp. 155–75

Clare, L., Roth, I. and Pratt, R. (2005) 'Perceptions of change over time in early-stage Alzheimer's disease', *Dementia*, Vol. 4, No. 4, pp. 487–520

Clarke, C. L. (1999) 'Dementia care partnerships: knowledge, ownership and exchange', in Adams, T. and Clarke, C. L. (eds) (1999) *Dementia Care: Developing Partnerships in Practice*, London: Ballière Tindall

Clarke, C. L. (2000) 'Risk: constructing care and care environments in dementia', *Health, Risk & Society*, Vol. 2, No. 1, pp. 83–93

Clough, R. *et al.* (2007) *The Support Older People Want and the Services They Need*, York: Joseph Rowntree Foundation

Cobban, N. (2004) 'Improving domiciliary care for people with dementia and their carers: the Raising the Standard project', in Innes, A., Archibald, C. and Murphy, C. (eds) (2004) *Dementia and Social Inclusion*, London: Jessica Kingsley

Commission for Health Improvement Investigations (2003) *Investigation into Matters Arising from Care on Rowan Ward, Manchester Health and Social Care Trust*, London: CHI

Cook, A. (2002) 'Using video to include the experiences of people with dementia in research', in Wilkinson, H. (ed.) (2002) *The Perspectives of People with Dementia*, London: Jessica Kingsley

Cook, A. (2003) 'Understanding the communication of older people with dementia living in residential care', PhD Thesis, University of Stirling

Cook, A., Niven, C. and Downs, M. (1999) 'Assessing the pain of people with cognitive impairments', *International Journal of Geriatric Psychiatry*, Vol. 14, pp. 421–5

Cook, A., Miller, E. and Whoriskey, M. (2007) *Do Health and Social Care Partnerships Deliver Good Outcomes to Service Users and Carers? Development of the User Defined Service Evaluation Toolkit*, Edinburgh: Joint Improvement Team

Cox, S. and Cook, A. (2002) 'Caring for people with dementia at the end of life', in Hockey, J. and Clark, D. (eds) (2002) *Ending Life in Institutional Care*, Open University Press, Milton Keynes

Craig, C. (2004) 'Reaching out with the arts: meeting the person with dementia', in Innes, A., Archibald, C. and Murphy, C. (eds) (2004) *Dementia and Social Inclusion*, London: Jessica Kingsley

Curtice, L. *et al.* (2002) *Over the Threshold? An exploration of intensive domiciliary support for older people*, Edinburgh: Scottish Executive

Dabbs, C. (1999) *'Please Knock and Come in for Some Tea': The views of people with dementia and improving their quality of life*, Preston: Preston Community Health Council

De Vries, K. (2003) 'Palliative care for people with dementia', in Adams, T. and Manthorpe, J. (eds) (2003) *Dementia Care*, London: Arnold

Dementia Services Development Centre (2007) *The Forth Valley Dementia Project*, University of Stirling

Department of Health (1989) White Paper, *Caring for People*, London: TSO

Department of Health (1998) *Modernising Adult Social Care Services*, London: TSO

Department of Health (1999) *National Service Framework for Mental Health*, London: TSO

Department of Health (2001) *National Service Framework for Older People*, London: TSO

Department of Health (2005a) *Independence, Well-being and Choice*, London: TSO

Department of Health (2005b) *Mental Capacity Act*, London: TSO

Department of Health (2006) *Our Health, Our Care, Our Say*, London: TSO

Department of Health (2007a) *Our NHS, Our Future*, London, TSO

Department of Health (2007b) 'Using practice-based commissioning to facilitate joined up working between health and social care' (online). Available from URL: www.dh.gov. uk/en/Managingyourorganisation/Commissioning/Practice-basedcommissioning/ DH_4131819 (accessed 21 July 2008)

Department of Health (2008a) *Putting People First*, London: Department of Health

Department of Health (2008b) *Transforming the Quality of Dementia Care*, London: Department of Health

Department of Health / Care Services Improvement Partnership (CSIP) (2005) *Everybody's Business: Integrated mental health services for older adults. A service development guide*, London: Department of Health

Dewing, J. (2002) 'From ritual to relationship: a person-centred approach to consent in qualitative research with older people who have dementia', *Dementia*, Vol. 1, No. 2, pp. 157–71

Dewing, J. (2006) 'Wandering into the future: reconceptualising wandering "a natural and good thing"', *International Journal of Older People Nursing*, Vol. 1, No. 4, pp. 239–49

Downs, M. *et al.* (2002) 'What do general practitioners tell people with dementia and their families about the condition? A survey of experiences in Scotland', *Dementia*, Vol. 1, No. 1, pp. 47–58

Droes, R.- M. *et al.* (2006) 'Quality of life in dementia in perspective: an explorative study of variations in opinions among people with dementia and their professional caregivers, and in literature', *Dementia*, Vol. 5, No. 4, pp. 533–58

Duncan-Myers, A. M. and Huebner, R. A. (2000) 'Relationship between choice and quality of life among residents in long-term care facilities', *American Journal of Occupational Therapy*, Vol. 54, pp. 504–8

Eckersley, R. (2008) 'What is well-being and what promotes it? The well-being manifesto' (online). Available from URL: www.wellbeingmanifesto.net/wellbeing.htm#_ednref2 (accessed 1 May 2008)

Estes, C. L. (1979) *The Aging Enterprise*, San Francisco: Jossey-Bass

Estes, C. L. (2001) *Social Policy and Aging: A critical perspective*, Thousand Oaks California: Sage Publications

Featherstone, M. and Hepworth, M. (1991) 'The mask of ageing', in Featherstone, M., Hepworth, M. and Turner, B. (eds) (1991) *The Body: Social process and cultural theory*, London: Sage

Fisk, M. and Abbott, S. (1998) 'Older people and the meaning of independence', *Generation Review* (Journal of the British Society of Gerontology), Vol. 8, No. 2, pp. 9–10

Forbat, L. (2005) *Talking about Care: Two sides to the story*, Bristol: The Policy Press

Foucault, M. (1977) *Discipline and Punish: The birth of the prison*, London: Allen Lane

Galloway, S. (2006) *Quality of Life and Well-being: Measuring the benefits of culture and sport. A Literature Review*, Edinburgh: Scottish Government

Gilleard, C. and Higgs, P. (2000) *Cultures of Ageing: Self, citizen and the body*, London: Prentice Hall

Gilliard, J. *et al.* (2005) 'Dementia care in England and the social model of disability', *Dementia*, Vol. 4, No. 4, pp. 571–86

Gilmour, H., Gibson, F. and Campbell J. (2003) 'Living alone with dementia', *Dementia*, Vol. 2, No. 3, pp. 403–20

Glasby, J. and Littlechild, R. (2006) 'An overview of the implementation and development of direct payments', in Leece, J. and Bornat, J. (eds.) (2006) *Developments in Direct Payments*, Bristol: Policy Press

Godfrey, M., Townsend, J. and Denby, T. (2004) *Building a Good Life for Older People in Local Communities*, York: Joseph Rowntree Foundation

Godlove, C., Richard, L. and Rodwell, G. (1982) *Time for Action: An observational study of elderly people in four different care environments*, Social Services Monographs, Research in Practice, Joint Unit for Social Services Research and Community Care, University of Sheffield

Goffman, E. (1963) *Stigma: Notes on the management of a spoiled identity*, Englewood Cliffs, N.J.: Prentice-Hall Inc.

Golander, H. and Raz, A. E. (1996) 'The mask of dementia: images of "demented residents" in a nursing ward', *Ageing and Society*, Vol. 16, pp. 269–85

Goldsmith, M. (1999) 'Ethical Dilemmas', in Adams, T. and Clarke, C. (eds) *Dementia Care: Developing partnerships in practice*, London: Ballière Tindall

Gubrium, J. F. (1975) *Living and Dying at Murray Manor*, New York: St Martin's Press

Gubrium, J. F. (1986) *Oldtimers and Alzheimer's: The descriptive organization of senility*, Greenwich, CT: JAI Press

Gwyther, L, P (1997) 'The perspective of the person with Alzheimer disease: which outcomes matter in early to middle stages of dementia?' *Alzheimer Disease and Associated Disorders*, Vol. 11, Suppl. 6, pp. 18–24

Haas, Barbara K. (1999) 'A multidisciplinary concept analysis of quality of life', *Western Journal of Nursing Research*, Vol. 21, No. 6, p. 728–42

Hasler, F. (2006) 'Holding the dream: direct payments and independent living', in Leece, J. and Bornat, J. (eds) (2006), *Developments in Direct Payments*, Bristol: Policy Press

Hazan, H. (1994) *Old Age: Constructions and deconstructions*, Cambridge: Cambridge University Press

Heller, T. and Heller, L. (2003) 'First among equals? Does drug treatment for dementia claim more than its fair share of resources?', *Dementia*, Vol. 2, No. 1, pp. 7–19

Help the Aged (2006) *My Home Life: Quality of Care in Care Homes*, London: Help the Aged

HM Government (2008) *Carers at the Heart of 21st Century Families and Communities: A caring system on your side, a life of your own*, London: Department of Health

Holden, U. and Stokes, G. (2002) 'The "Dementias"', in Stokes, G. and Goudie, F. (eds) (2002) *The Essential Dementia Care Handbook*, Bicester: Speechmark

Holmes, C., Cooper, B. and Levy, R. (1995) 'Dementia known to mental health services: first findings of a case register for a defined elderly population', *International Journal of Geriatric Psychiatry*, Vol. 10, pp. 871–81

Hubbard, G., Downs, M. and Tester, S. (2002a) 'Including the perspectives of older people in institutional care, including residents unable to give informed consent, during the consent process', in Wilkinson, H. (ed.) (2002), *The Perspectives of People with Dementia*, London: Jessica Kingsley

Hubbard, G. *et al.* (2002b) 'Beyond words: older people with dementia using and interpreting non-verbal behaviour', *Journal of Aging Studies*, Vol. 16, pp. 155–67

Hubbard, G., Tester, S. and Downs M. (2003) 'Meaningful social interactions between older people in institutional care settings', *Ageing and Society*, Vol. 23, pp. 99–114

Hudson, B. (2007) 'What lies ahead for partnership working? Collaborative contexts and policy tensions', *Journal of Integrated Care*, Vol. 15, No. 3, pp. 29–36

Hughes, D (2002) 'Bauman's strangers: impairment and the invalidation of disabled people in modern and post-modern culture', *Disability and Society*, Vol. 17, No. 5, pp. 571–84

Hughes, J. C., Louw, S. J. and Sabat, S. R. (eds) (2006) *Dementia: Mind, meaning and the person*, Oxford: Oxford University Press

Hulko, W. (2002) 'Making the links: social theories, experiences of people with dementia and intersectionality', in Leibing, A. and Scheinkman, L. (eds) (2002), *The Diversity of Alzheimer's Disease: Different approaches and contexts*, Rio de Janiero: CUCA-IPUB

Hulko, W. (2008) 'From "not a big deal" to "hellish": experiences of older people with dementia', *Journal of Ageing Studies*

Information and Statistics Division (2006) *SPARRA: Scottish Patients at Risk of Readmission and Admission*, Edinburgh: ISD

Joint Future Unit (2007) *National Outcomes for Community Care*, Scottish Executive

Joint Improvement Team (2008) *Telecare Development Programme News, July 2008*: Joint Improvement Team

Katsuno, T. (2005) 'Dementia from the inside: how people with early-stage dementia evaluate their quality of life', *Ageing and Society*, Vol. 25, pp. 197–214

Keady, J. and Gilliard, J. (1999) 'The early experience of Alzheimer's disease: implications for partnership and practice', in Adams, T. and Clarke, C. (eds) (1999), *Dementia Care: Developing partnerships in practice*, London: Ballière Tindall

Killick, J. and Allan, K. (2001) *Communication and the Care of People with Dementia*, Buckingham: Open University Press

Kings Fund (2007) *Briefing: Practice Based Commissioning*, London: Kings Fund

Kitwood, T. (1987) 'Explaining senile dementia: the limits of neuropathological research', *Free Associations,* Vol. 10, pp. 117–40

Kitwood, T. (1997) *Dementia Reconsidered,* Buckingham: Open University Press

Kitwood, T. and Bredin, K. (1992) 'A new approach to the evaluation of dementia care', *Journal of Advances in Health and Nursing Care,* Vol. 1, No. 5, pp. 41–60

Knapp, M. *et al.* (2007) *Dementia UK: Report to the Alzheimer's Society,* Kings College London and London School of Economics and Political Science

Kumpers, S. *et al.* (2005) 'A comparative study of dementia care in England and the Netherlands using neo-institutionalist perspectives', *Qualitative Health Research,* Vol. 15, No. 9, pp. 1199–230

Leece, J. and Bornat, J. (eds) (2006) *Developments in Direct Payments,* Bristol: Policy Press

Mace, N. and Rabins, P. (2006) *The 36 Hour Day: A family guide to caring for persons with Alzheimer's disease, related dementing illnesses and memory loss in later life,* New York: Warner Books

Magai, C. *et al.* (1996) 'Emotional expression during mid- to late-stage dementia', *International Psychogeriatrics,* Vol. 8, No. 3, pp. 383–95

Manthorpe, J. (2004) 'Risk taking', in Innes, A., Archibald, C. and Murphy, C. (eds) (2004) *Dementia and Social Inclusion,* London: Jessica Kingsley

Manthorpe, J., Iliffe, S. and Eden, A. (2003) 'Early recognition of dementia by nurses', *Journal of Advanced Nursing,* Vol. 44, No. 2, pp. 183–91

Marshall, M. (1997) *State of the Art in Dementia Care,* London, UK: Centre for Policy on Ageing

Marshall, M. and Tibbs, M.- A. (2006) *Social Work and People with Dementia,* Bristol: Policy Press

Mason, A. and Wilkinson, H. (2002) *The Characteristics of People with Dementia who are Users and Non Users of the Legal System,* Edinburgh: Scottish Executive

McClean, W. and Cunningham, C. (2007) *Pain in Older People and People with Dementia,* Stirling: Dementia Services Development Centre

McColgan, G. (2001) '"They come here to tangle": An ethnographic study of relationships of people with dementia', PhD Thesis, University of Stirling

McColgan, G., Valentine, J. and Downs, M. (2000) 'Concluding narratives of a career with dementia: accounts of Iris Murdoch at her death', *Ageing and Society,* Vol. 20, No. 1, pp. 97–109

McCormack, D. and Whitehead, A. (1981) 'The effect of providing recreational activities on the engagement levels of long-stay geriatric patients', *Age and Ageing,* Vol. 10, No. 4, pp. 287–91

McGrath, A. and Jackson, G. (1996) 'Survey of neuroleptic prescribing in residents of nursing homes in Glasgow', *British Medical Journal,* Vol. 312, pp. 611–12

McKillop, J. (2002) 'Did research alter anything?', in Wilkinson, H. (ed.) (2002)*The Perspectives of People with Dementia,* London: Jessica Kingsley

Medical Research Council (2000) 'Good research practice' (online). Available from URL: www.mrc.ac.uk (accessed 8 February 2003)

Melzer, D. *et al.* (2004) 'Alzheimer's disease and other dementias', in Stevens, A. and Rafferty, J. (eds) *Health Care Needs Assessment: The epidemiologically based needs assessment reviews (1ˢᵗ series).* Available from URL: http://hcna.radcliffe-oxford.com/ dementiaframe.htm

Mental Welfare Commission for Scotland (2006) *Older and Wiser,* Edinburgh: Mental Welfare Commission for Scotland

Mentis, M., Briggs-Whittaker, J. and Gramigna, G. D. (1995) 'Discourse topic management in senile dementia of the Alzheimer's type', *Journal of Speech and Hearing Research,* Vol. 38, pp. 1054–66

Mills, M. (2003) 'A meeting of minds: allowing older people with dementia to share their thoughts and experiences about health and social care, using counselling skills',

Research Policy and Planning, Vol. 21, No. 2, pp. 33–42

Moïse, P., Schwarzinger, M and Um, M.-Y. (2004) *Dementia Care in 9 OECD Countries: A comparative analysis*, OECD Directorate for Employment, Labour and Social Affairs

Moran, J. (2001) 'Ageing and identity in dementia narratives', *Cultural Values*, Vol. 5, No. 2, pp. 245–60

Moriarty, J. and Webb, S. (2000) *Part of Their Lives: Community care for older people with dementia*, Bristol: The Policy Press

Morris, J. (2006) 'Independent living: the role of the disability movement in the development of government policy', in Glendinning, C. and Kemp, P. (eds) (2006) *Cash and Care: Policy challenges in the welfare state*, Bristol: Policy Press

Moyle, W. *et al.* (2007) 'Quality of life and dementia: the voice of the person with dementia', *Dementia*, Vol. 7, No. 2, pp. 175–91

National Audit Office (2007) *Improving Services and Support for People with Dementia*, London: The Stationery Office

National Institute for Health and Clinical Excellence/ Social Care Institute for Excellence (2006) *Dementia: Supporting People with Dementia and their Carers in Health and Social Care*, National Institute for Health and Clinical Excellence

Norberg, A., Melin, E. and Asplund, K. (1986) 'Reactions to music, touch and object presentation in the final stage of dementia: an exploratory study', *International Journal of Nursing Studies*, Vol. 23, No. 4, pp. 315–23

O'Brien, M. and Penna, S. (1998) *Theorising Welfare: Enlightenment and modern society*, London: Sage

Old Spice Drama Group (2003) *Presentation to the 32nd Annual conference of the British Society of Gerontology*, Newcastle 4–6 September

Oldman, C. and Quilgars, D. (1999) 'The last resort? Revisiting ideas about older people's living arrangements', *Ageing and Society*, Vol. 19, pp. 363–84

Oliver, M. (1990) *The Politics of Disablement*, Basingstoke: Macmillan

Palo-Bengtsson, L. and Ekman, S. L. (1997) 'Social dancing in the care of persons with dementia in a nursing home setting: a phenomenological study', *Scholarly Inquiry for Nursing Practice*, Vol. 11, No. 2, pp. 101–18

Papastavrou, E. *et al.* (2007) 'Caring for a relative with dementia: family caregiver burden', *Journal of Advanced Nursing*, Vol. 58, No. 5, pp. 446–57

Paterniti, D (2000) 'The micropolitics of identity in adverse circumstances. A study of identity making in a total institution', *Journal of Contemporary Ethnography*, Vol. 29, No. 1, pp. 93–119

Paulson, S. (2003) 'The social construction of ageing in a dance/movement group', *Paper presented to the 32nd Annual Conference of the British Society of Gerontology, Newcastle 4–6 September*

Peace, S. and Holland, C. (2002) *Inclusive Housing in an Ageing Society: Innovative approaches*, Bristol: Policy Press

Peace, S., Kellaher, L. and Wilcocks, D. (1997) *Re-evaluating Residential Care*, Buckinghamshire: Open University Press

Pearson, C. (2006) 'Direct payments in Scotland', in J. Leece, J. and Bornat, J. (eds), (2006), *Developments in Direct Payments*, Bristol: Policy Press

Petch, A. (2007) *Health and Social Care: Establishing a Joint Future?*, Edinburgh: Dunedin Academic Press

Petch, A. *et al.* (2007) *Users and Carers Define Effective Partnerships in Health and Social Care*, University of Glasgow

Phillipson, C. (1998) *Reconstructing Old Age: New agendas in social theory and practice*, London: Sage Publications

Plummer, K. (2001) *Documents of Life 2: An invitation to critical humanism*, London: Sage

Post, S. (2000) *The Moral Challenge of Alzheimer Disease*, Baltimore: Johns Hopkins Press

Pratt, R. and Wilkinson, H. (2003) 'A psychosocial model of understanding the experience of receiving a diagnosis of dementia', *Dementia,* Vol. 2, No. 2, pp. 181–99

Quayhagen, M. P. and Quayhagen, M. (1996) 'Discovering life quality in coping with dementia', *Western Journal of Nursing Research,* Vol.18, No. 2, pp. 120–35

Ready, R. E. and Ott, B. R. (2003) 'Quality of life measures for dementia', *Health and Quality of Life Outcomes,* Vol. 1

Reed, J., Roskell Payton, V. and Bond, S. (1998) 'The importance of place for older people moving into care homes', *Social Science and Medicine,* Vol. 46, No. 7, pp. 859–67

Reeve, D. (2002) 'Negotiating psycho-emotional dimensions of disability and their influence on identity constructions', *Disability and Society,* Vol. 17, No. 5, pp. 493–508

Reid, D., Ryan, T. and Enderby, P. (2001) 'What does it mean to listen to people with dementia', *Disability and Society,* Vol. 16, No. 3, pp. 377–92

Ridley, J. and Jones, L. (2003) 'Direct what? The untapped potential of direct payments to mental health service users', *Disability and Society,* Vol. 18, No. 5, pp. 643–58

Ritchie, K. and Lovestone, S. (2002) 'The dementias', *The Lancet,* Vol. 360, No. 9347, pp. 1759–66

Robinson, E. (2002) 'Should people with Alzheimer's disease take part in research?', in Wilkinson, H. (ed.) (2002), *The Perspectives of People with Dementia,* London: Jessica Kingsley

Rosenstrom Chang, L. *et al.* (2006) 'Environmental scan', in Slote Morris, Z. *et al.* (eds) (2006), *Policy Futures for UK Health,* Oxford: Radcliffe Publishing

Sabat, S. R. (2001) *The Experience of Alzheimer's Disease: Life through a tangled veil,* Oxford: Blackwell

Sargeant, E. (2008) *Creative Models of Short Breaks (Respite Care) for People with Dementia,* London: Care Services Improvement Partnership

Scottish Executive (2000) *Adults with Incapacity Act,* Edinburgh: Scottish Executive

Scottish Executive (2002) *Adding Life to Years: Report of the Expert Group on Healthcare of Older People,* Edinburgh: Scottish Executive

Scottish Executive (2004) *HDL 44 Template for Dementia Services,* Edinburgh: Scottish Executive

Scottish Executive (2005) *Better Outcomes for Older People,* Edinburgh: Scottish Executive

Scottish Executive (2006a) *Changing Lives: Report of the 21st century Social Work Review,* Edinburgh: Scottish Executive

Scottish Executive (2006b) *Delivering for Mental Health,* Edinburgh: Scottish Executive

Scottish Executive (2007) *All Our Futures: Planning for a Scotland with an ageing population,* Edinburgh: Scottish Executive

Scottish Executive / NHS Scotland (2005) *Building a Health Service Fit for the Future,* Edinburgh: Scottish Executive

Scottish Government (2007a) *Better Health, Better Care,* Edinburgh: Scottish Government

Scottish Government (2007b) *Towards a Mentally Flourishing Scotland,* Edinburgh: Scottish Government

Scottish Intercollegiate Network Guidelines (2006) *Guideline 86: Management of Patients with Dementia,* Edinburgh: NHS QIS

Shaw, M. et al. (1999) *The Widening Gap: Health inequalities and policy in Britain,* The Policy Press: Bristol

Snyder, L. (1999) *Speaking our Minds: Personal reflections from individuals with Alzheimer's,* New York: W H Freeman and Company

Sterin, G. (2002) 'Essay on a word: a lived experience of Alzheimer's disease', *Dementia,* Vol. 1, No. 1, pp. 7–10

Stewart, A. (2006) 'How direct payments changed my life', in Leece, J. and Bornat, J.

(eds.) (2006) *Developments in Direct Payments*, Bristol: Policy Press

Townsend, P. (1962) *The Last Refuge*, London: Routledge and Kegan Paul

Townsend, P. (1981) 'The structured dependency of the elderly: the creation of social policy in the 20th century', *Ageing and Society*, Vol. 1, No. 1, pp. 5–28

Turner, S. *et al.* (2004) 'General practitioners' knowledge, confidence and attitudes in the diagnosis and management of dementia', *Age and Ageing*, Vol. 33, pp. 461–67

Tyrrell, J., Genin, N. and Myslinski, M. (2006) 'Freedom of choice and decision-making in health and social care: views of older patients with early-stage dementia and their carers', *Dementia*, Vol. 5, No. 4, pp. 479–502

Vernooji-Dassen *et al.* (2005) 'Factors affecting timely recognition and diagnosis of dementia across Europe: from awareness to stigma', *International Journal of Geriatric Psychiatry*, Vol. 20, pp. 377–86

Walker, A. (1981) 'Towards a political economy of old age', *Ageing and Society*, Vol. 1, No. 1, pp. 73–94

Walker, A. (1997) 'Introduction: the strategy of inequality', in Walker, A. and Walker, C. (eds) (1997), *Britain Divided: The growth of social exclusion in the 1980s and 1990s*, London: Child Poverty Action Group

Walker, A. (1999) 'Public policy and theories of aging', in Bengtson, V. J. and Schaie, K. W. (eds) (1999), *Handbook of theories of aging*, New York: Springer

Wanless, D. (2006) *Securing Good Care for Older People: Taking a long-term view*, London: King's Fund

Watson, N. (2002) 'Well, I know this is going to sound very strange to you, but I don't see myself as a disabled person: identity and disability', *Disability and Society*, Vol. 17, No. 5, pp. 509–27

Weaks, D. (2006) 'Living within a limited freedom: the perceptions and experiences of early dementia from the perspectives of people with the diagnosis and the diagnosticians', Unpublished PhD Thesis, University of Abertay

Weaks, D. (2008) Personal communication

Weir, R. (2008) Personal communication

Whitehead M. and Dahlgren G. (1991) 'What can be done about inequalities in health?', *The Lancet*, Vol. 338, pp. 1059–63

Whitehouse, P. (1999) 'Quality of life in Alzheimer's disease: future directions', *Journal of Mental Health and Aging*, Vol. 5 No. 1, pp. 533–46

Whitehouse, P. *et al.* (1997) 'Quality of life assessment in dementia drug development', *Alzheimer's Disease and Associated Disorders*, Vol. 11, No. 3, pp. 56–60

Wilkinson, H. (ed.) (2002) *The Perspectives of People with Dementia*, Jessica Kingsley, London

Wilkinson, H. and McKillop, J. (2004) 'Make it easy on yourself! Advice to researchers from someone with dementia on being interviewed', *Dementia: The International Journal of Social Research*, Vol. 3, No. 2

Woods, B. and Pratt, R. (2005) 'Awareness in dementia: ethical and legal issues in relation to people with dementia', *Aging and Mental Health*, Vol. 9, No. 5, pp. 423–9

Woods, R. T. *et al.* (2003) 'Dementia: issues in early recognition and intervention in primary care', *Journal of the Royal Society of Medicine*, Vol. 96, pp. 320–4

Woolham, J., Gibson, G. and Clarke, P. (2006) 'Assistive technology, telecare and dementia: some implications of current policies and guidance', *Research Policy and Planning*, Vol. 24, No. 3, pp. 149–64

World Health Organization (2002) *Active Ageing: A policy framework*, Geneva: World Health Organization

Index